Virtuoso Harmonica Solos

by Jiayi He

Online Audio

www.melbay.com/30580MEB

www.melbay.com

Preface

Many harmonica players want to become virtuoso performers. However, there is a lack of good, advanced music scored for harmonica. The harmonica dates back less than 200 years so this is perhaps the reason for the lack of challenging, advanced solo material.

I have given concerts worldwide and am often asked for the arrangements I have performed. Many of the pieces I play have never been performed on the harmonica. It is my desire to share what I have learned with the many harmonica players wanting to reach a level of excellence in performance.

In order to improve my harmonica playing I have studied various other instruments. Certain string bowing techniques and breathing techniques utilized by wind instrument players can be adapted to the harmonica. I have performed such works as Sarasate's *Carmen Fantasy,* Liszt's *Hungarian Rhapsody No. 2*, Gershwin's *Rhapsody in Blue*, Bach's *Violin Concerto*,Vivaldi's *Double Concerto* and others with full orchestras. I teach these advanced pieces to my students at the *Turtle Bay Music School.*

I have included harmonica tabs with notes in this book. The tabs show the harmonica hole numbers, breath direction and slide positions. A *Special Scale Study Section* is added which presents the 12 Major and minor keys and the arpeggios related to each. An added feature is the inclusion of online recorded accompaniment tracks. These backup tracks will greatly aid practice and will help the harmonica player learn the solos contained in this book.

Jiayi He
Harmonica faculty of the Turtle Bay Music School
New York City
October 20, 2016

Table of Contents

Harmonica Holes, Numbers and Range

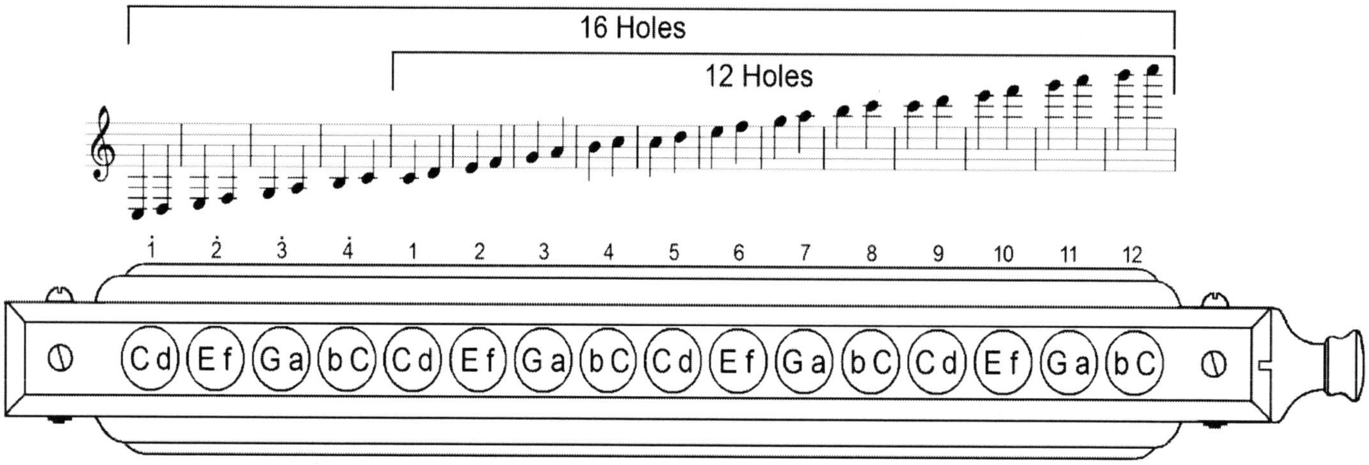

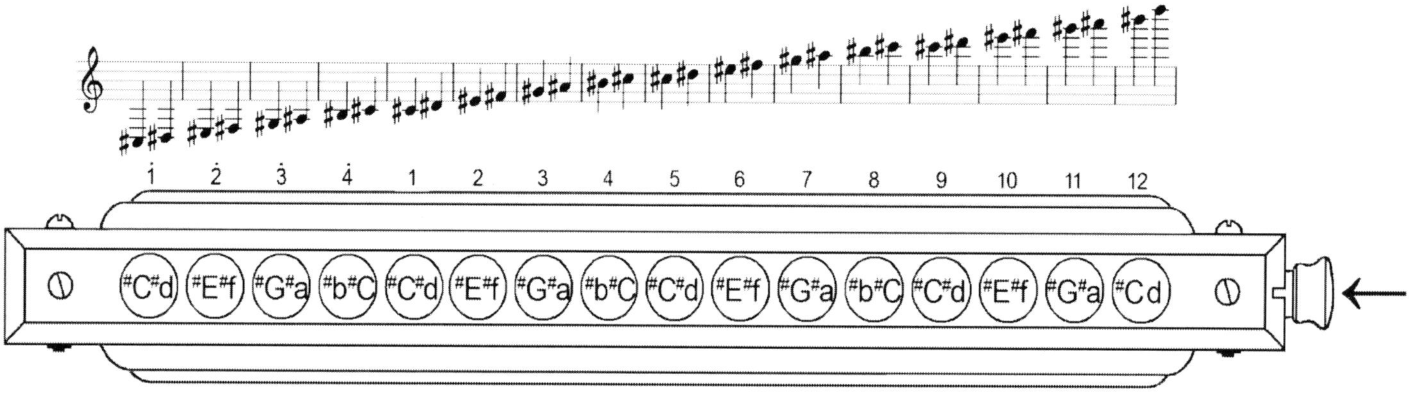

Uppercase letters (C - E - G - C# - E# - G#) = Blow

Lowercase letters (d - f - a - b - d# - f# - a# - b#) = Draw

About Harmonica Tabs

1. 1 to 12 are the hole numbers stamped on the harmonica.
2. The sign "V" above a note indicates to draw (inhale). If no sign exists you are to blow (exhale).
3. The sign ← above a note indicates to push the harmonica slide in.
4. ( ) indicates possible options for playing the note.
5. When two numbers are vertically placed together, meaning double stops or octaves, play both notes together at the same time. Octaves and some double stops use the tongue blocking technique to block off the middle notes between the two desired notes.
6. The small "cue" sized notes represent a prelude or interlude played by another instrument or orchestra and the harmonica will start playing when the normal sized notes appear.
7. To ascertain the position of all notes in all keys refer to the *Special Scale Study Section* on page 93.

Special Scale Study Section

About the Backing Tracks

Anitra's Dance:	Harmonica starts playing after a long note and 11 beats.
Arioso:	Harmonica starts playing after 4 beats.
Concerto No. 1 - I:	Harmonica starts playing the eighth-note on the second half of the 4th beat.
Concerto No. 1 - III:	Harmonica starts playing the eighth-note on the 9th beat after counting the 1st beat, 4th beat and 7th beat.
Carmen Fantasy - Gypsy Dance:	Harmonica starts playing after 6 beats.
Gavotte and Rondo:	This is an unaccompanied solo piece. There is no backing track.
Hungarian Dance No. 5:	Harmonica starts playing after 4 beats.
La Cinquantaine:	Harmonica starts playing the quarter-note on the second half of the 4th beat.
Minute Waltz:	Harmonica starts playing after additional Ab chord. Listen to the 1st beat of the 3rd measure. The harmonica should be at the correct tempo on the 1st beat of the 5th measure.
Violin Concerto in A minor - I:	Harmonica starts playing the eighth-note on the second half of the 4th beat.
Violin Concerto in A minor - II:	Harmonica starts playing after 4 beats.
Violin Concerto in A minor - III:	Harmonica starts playing the eighth-note on the second half of the 3rd beat.
Serenade:	Harmonica starts playing after three beats.

For the rest of the backing tracks the harmonica starts playing after the introductions.

12th Street Rag

Euday L. Bowman, Arr. Jiayi He

26
31
V 4 V 4 V 4 V 4 6 V 4 2
37
V 4 V 4 V 3 V 4
42
V 4
47
V 4 V 4 V 3 V 6 3 V 8 5

53
58
63
69
74

Anitra's Dance

Edward Grieg Arr. Jiayi He

rit
a tempo
gliss.
f
pp

This page has been left blank to avoid an awkward page turn.

Arioso

(From Cantata 156)

J. S. Bach, Arr. Jiayi He

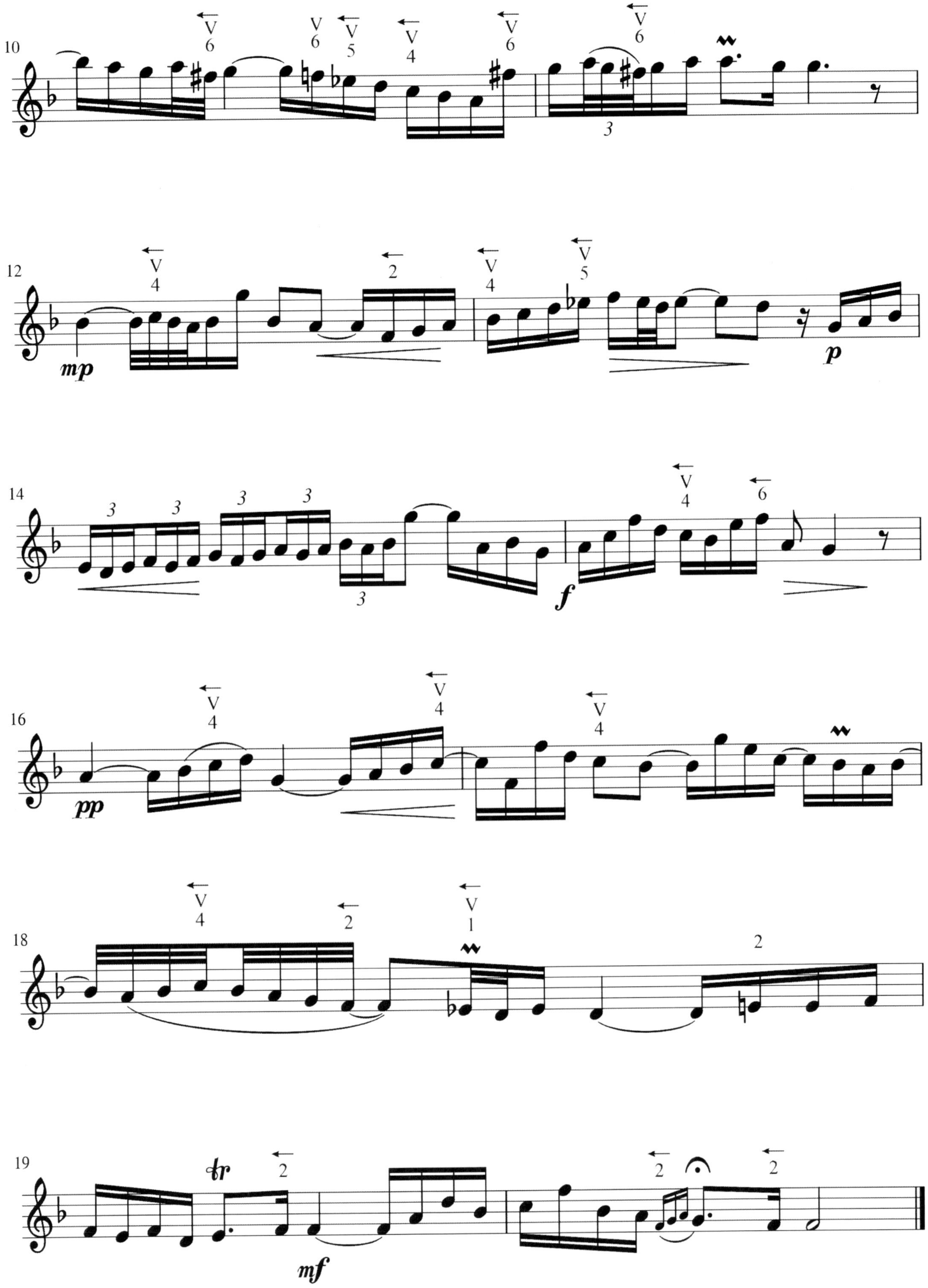

Violin Concerto No. 1

J. S. Bach, Arr. Jiayi He

I

Allegro moderato

32
36
40
B
mf
45
49
f
54
C
59

64
70
75
79
84
89
tr
D
f
mf
p

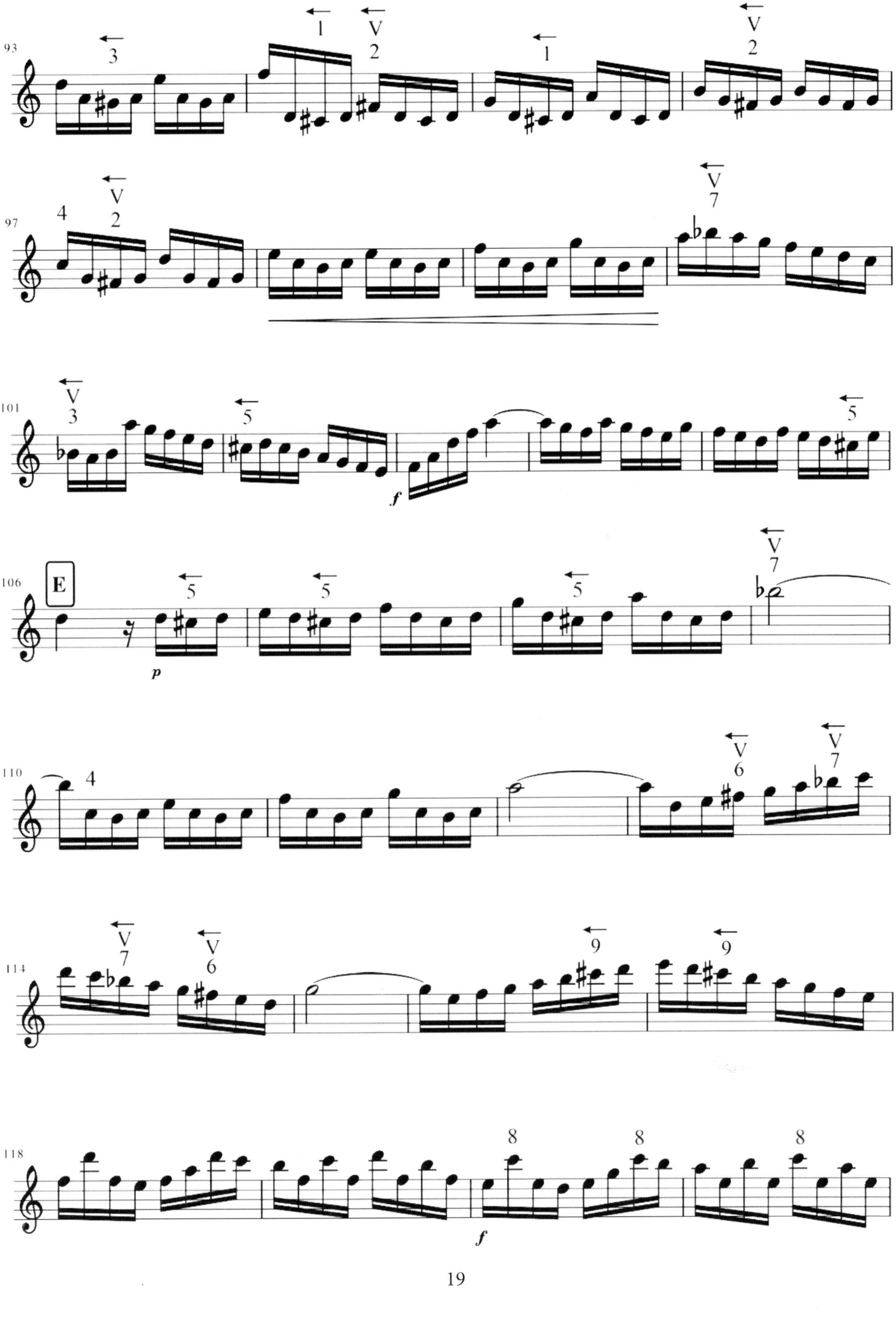
E

122
126
F
130
134
138
142

146
G
152
156
160
tr
dim
164
f
168
tr

Violin Concerto No. 1

II

J. S. Bach, Arr. Jiayi He

Andante

Violin Concerto No. 1

III

J. S. Bach, Arr. Jiayi He

Allegro assai

54
57
60
64
67
70

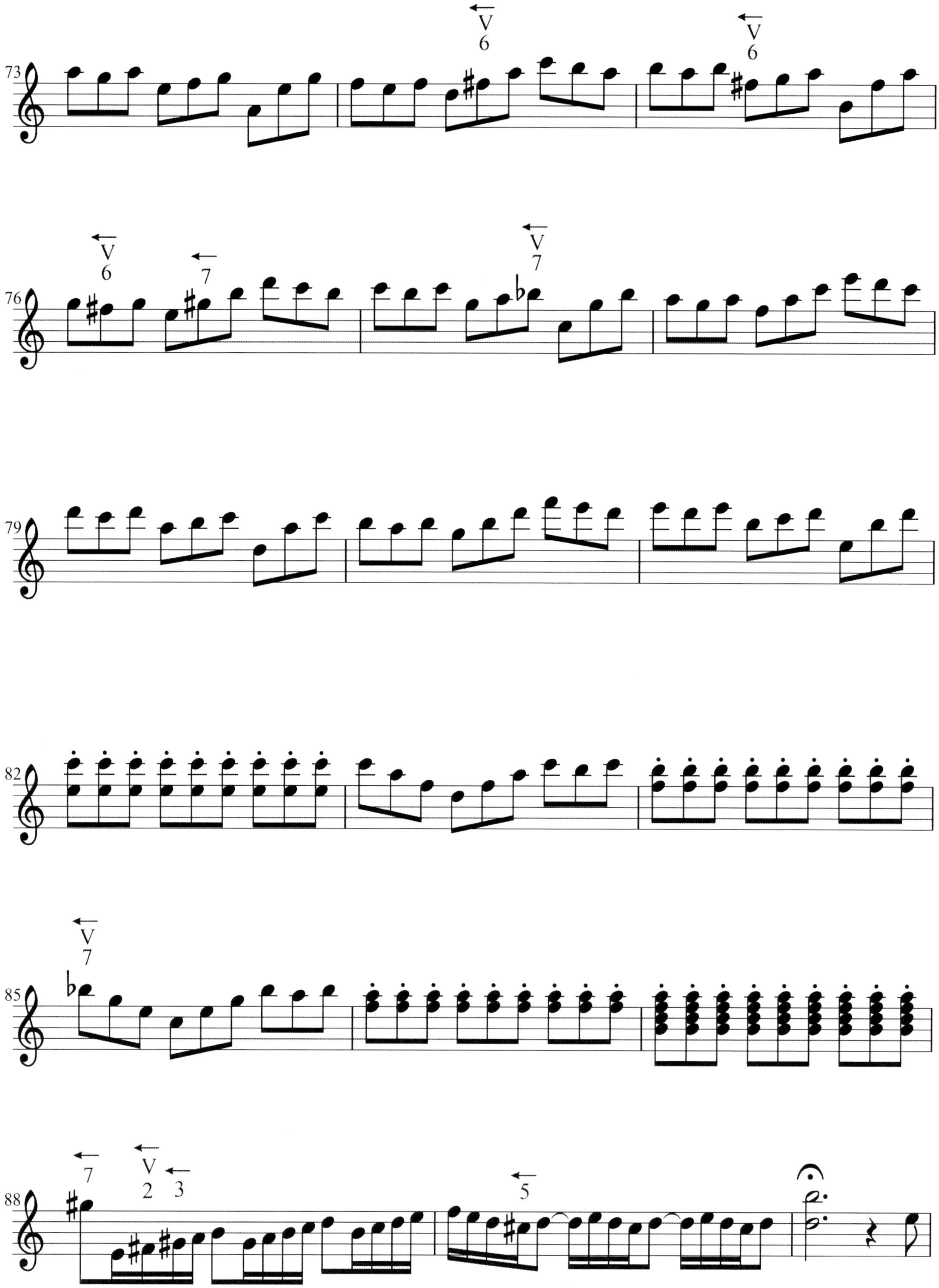

91
94
97
100
102
104

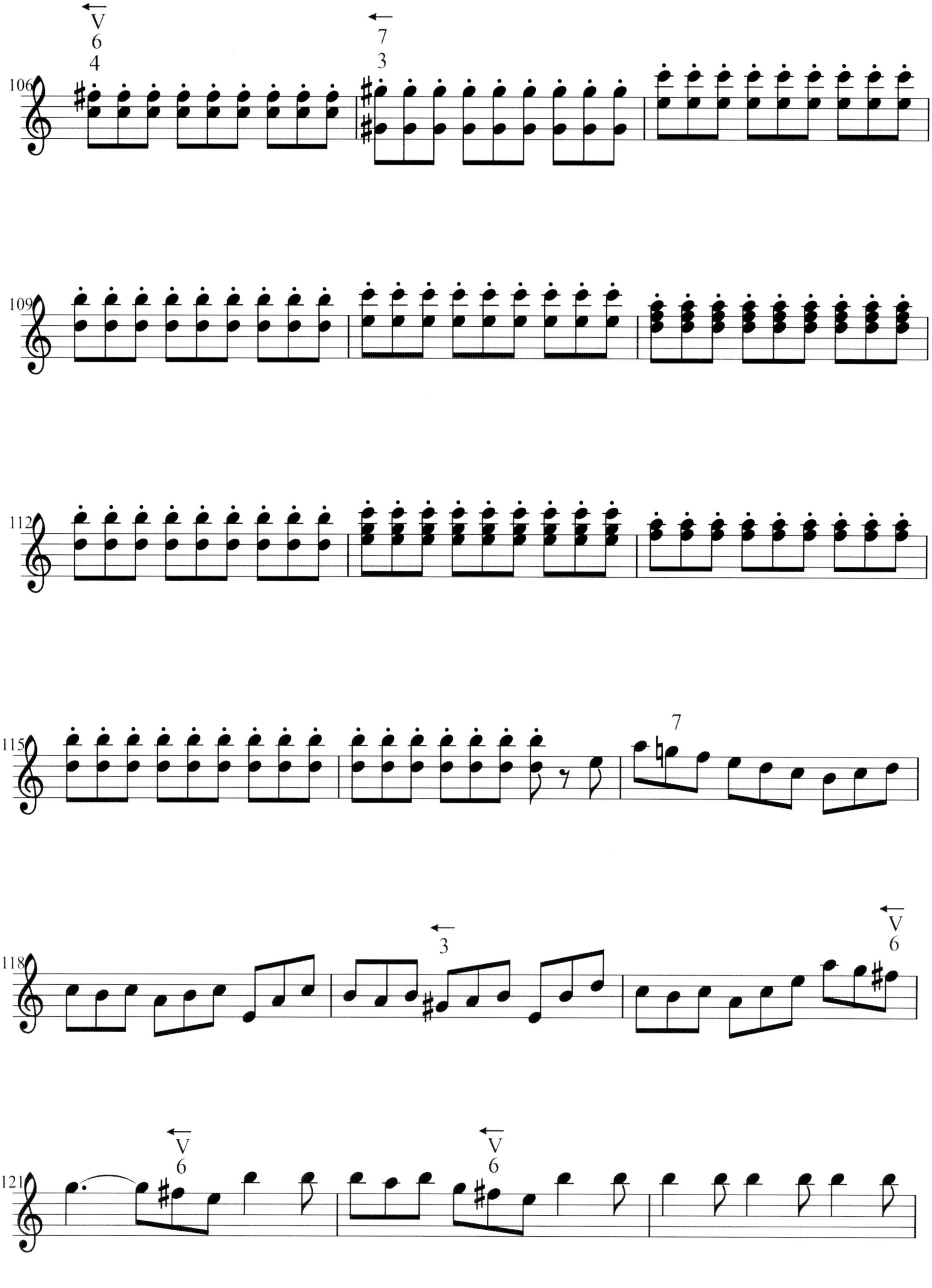
106
109
112
115
118
121

Aragonaise

Carmen Fantasy

Pablo Sarasate, Arr. Jiayi He

gliss.
gliss.
B
gliss.
gliss.
rit

C
rit

124
D
131
139
p
147
152
E
mf
159
gliss.
gliss.
tr
p
165
170
pp

Habanera

Carmen Fantasy

Pablo Sarasate, Arr. Jiayi He

C
D
f
p
ff

64
68
72
76
80
85
90
8va
(8va)
E
p
f

dim
dim
F

Interlude

Pablo Sarasate, Arr. Jiayi He

Carmen Fantasy

a tempo
8va
pp
(8va)
cresc.
ff
Tempo I
p

Seguidilla

Pablo Sarasate, Arr. Jiayi He

Carmen Fantasy

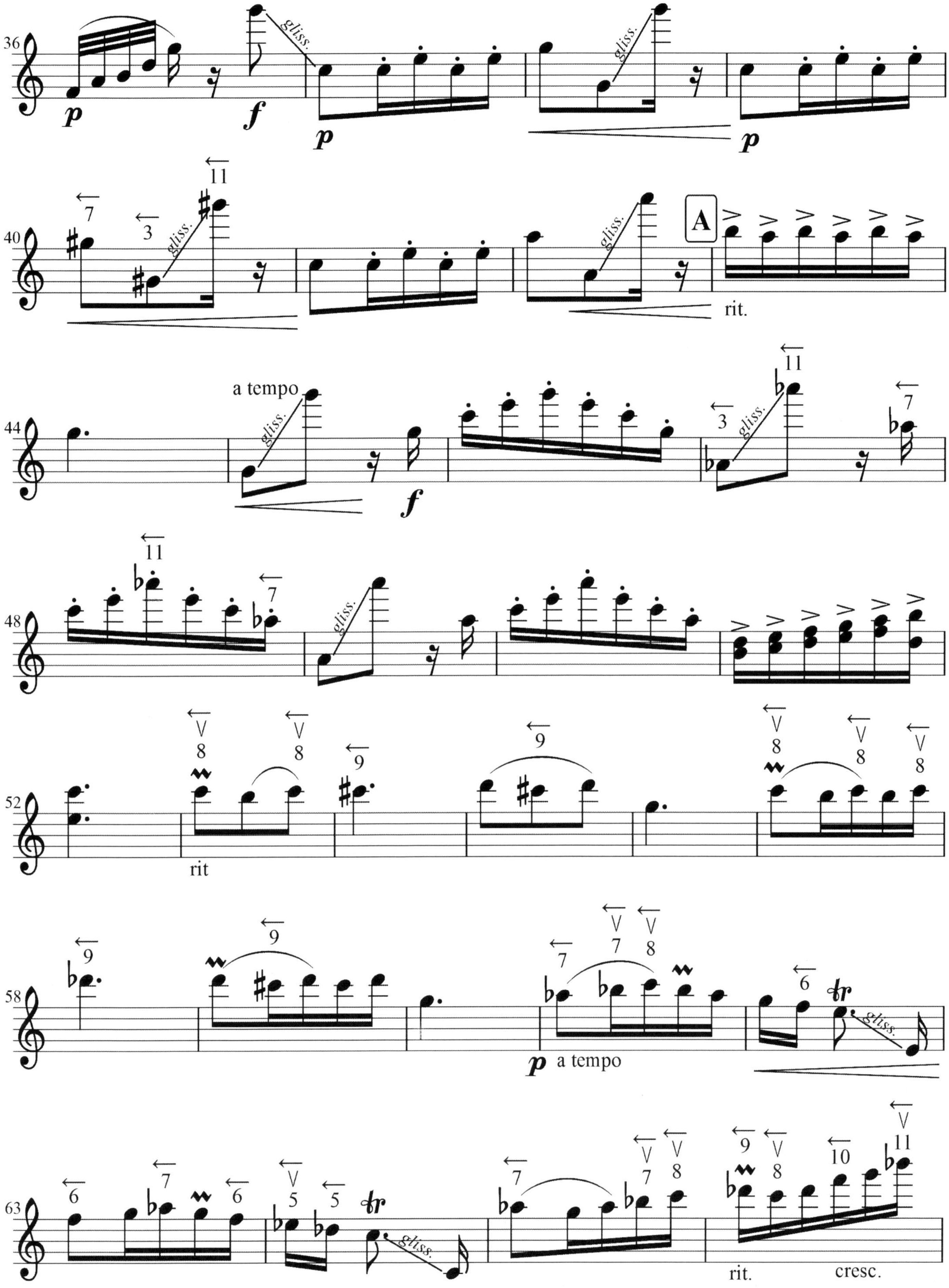
gliss.
p
f
rit.
a tempo
A
rit
cresc.

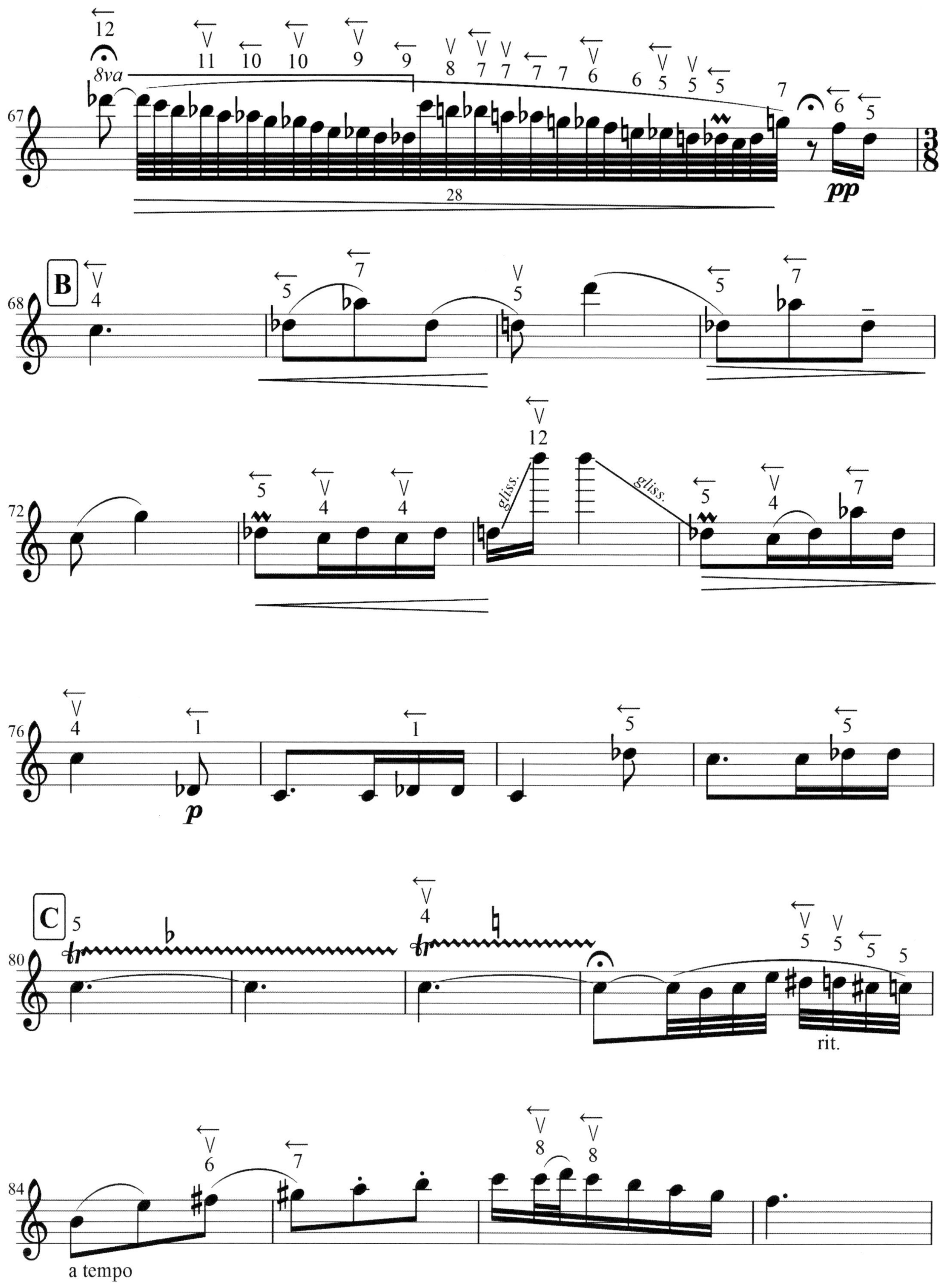
8va
pp
B
gliss.
gliss.
p
C
rit.
a tempo

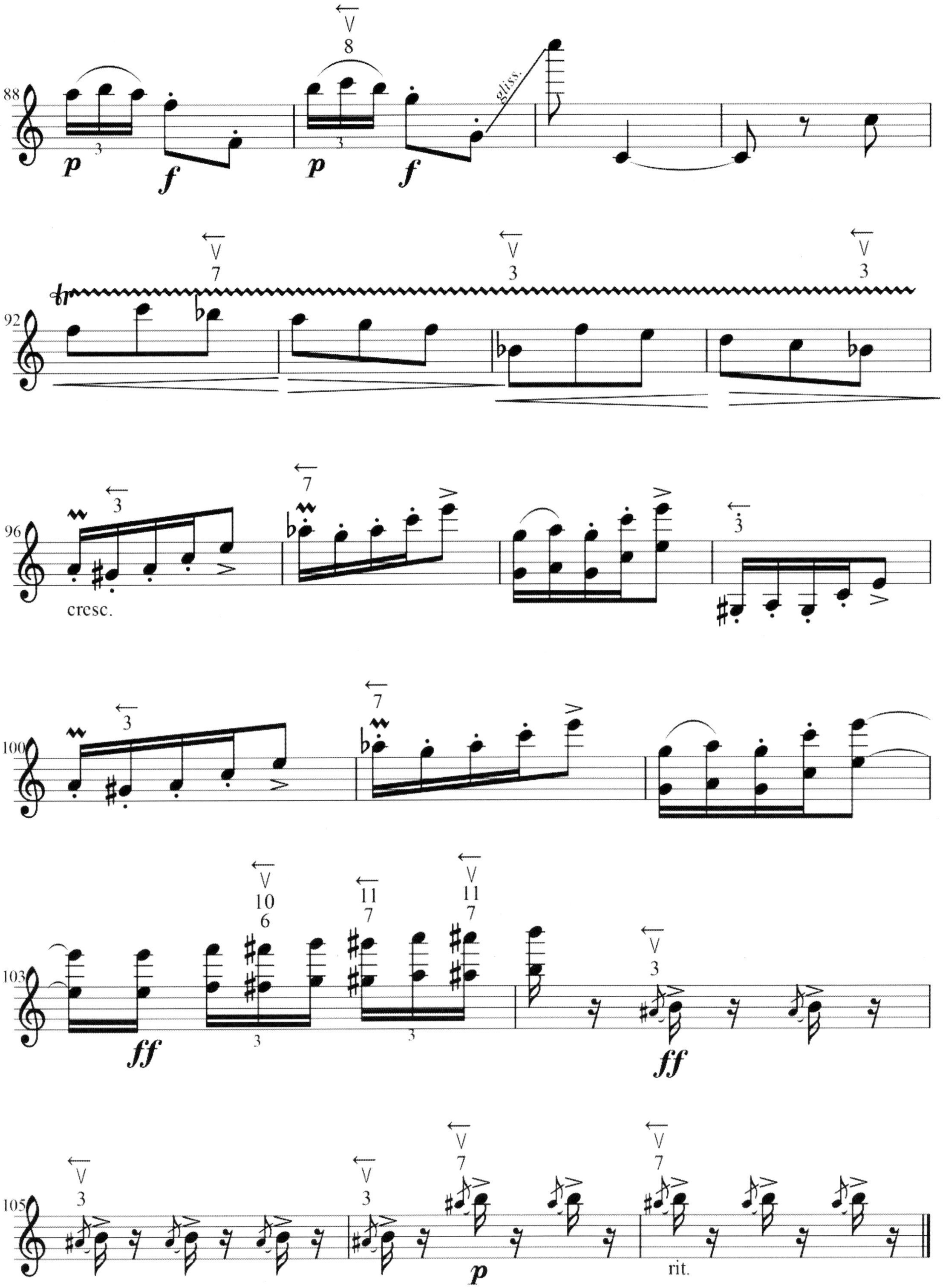
gliss.
cresc.
rit.

Gypsy Dance

Carmen Fantasy

Pablo Sarasate, Arr. Jiayi He

B
C
rit.
D
a tempo

a tempo
E

F
rit.
a tmepo
G
ff

Gavotte and Rondo

Unaccompanied Solo

J. S. Bach, Arr. Jiayi He

cresc.
cresc.
dim.

cresc.
cresc.
cresc.
rit.

Harmonica Wizard

John Philip Sousa, Arr. Jiayi He

ff
ff
1.
2.

Hungarian Dance No. 5

Johannes Brahms, Arr. Jiayi He

37
p
43
sf
48
f
54
61
poco rit
a tempo
poco rit
a tempo
p
68
poco rit
a tempo
poco rit
p

a tempo

La Cinquantaine

Gabriel Marie, Arr. Jiayi He

30
6
36
6
42
48
cresc.
V
5
V
1
53
1.
2.

58
pp
63
V
5
rit.
f
1.
2.
a tempo.
p
68
6
mf
73
tr
p
79
mf

Minute Waltz

Frederic Chopin, Arr. Jiayi He

cresc. poco a poco

Violin Concerto in A minor

I

Antonio Vivaldi, Arr. Jiayi He

Allegro

Violin Concerto in A minor

II

Antonio Vivaldi, Arr. Jiayi He

Largo

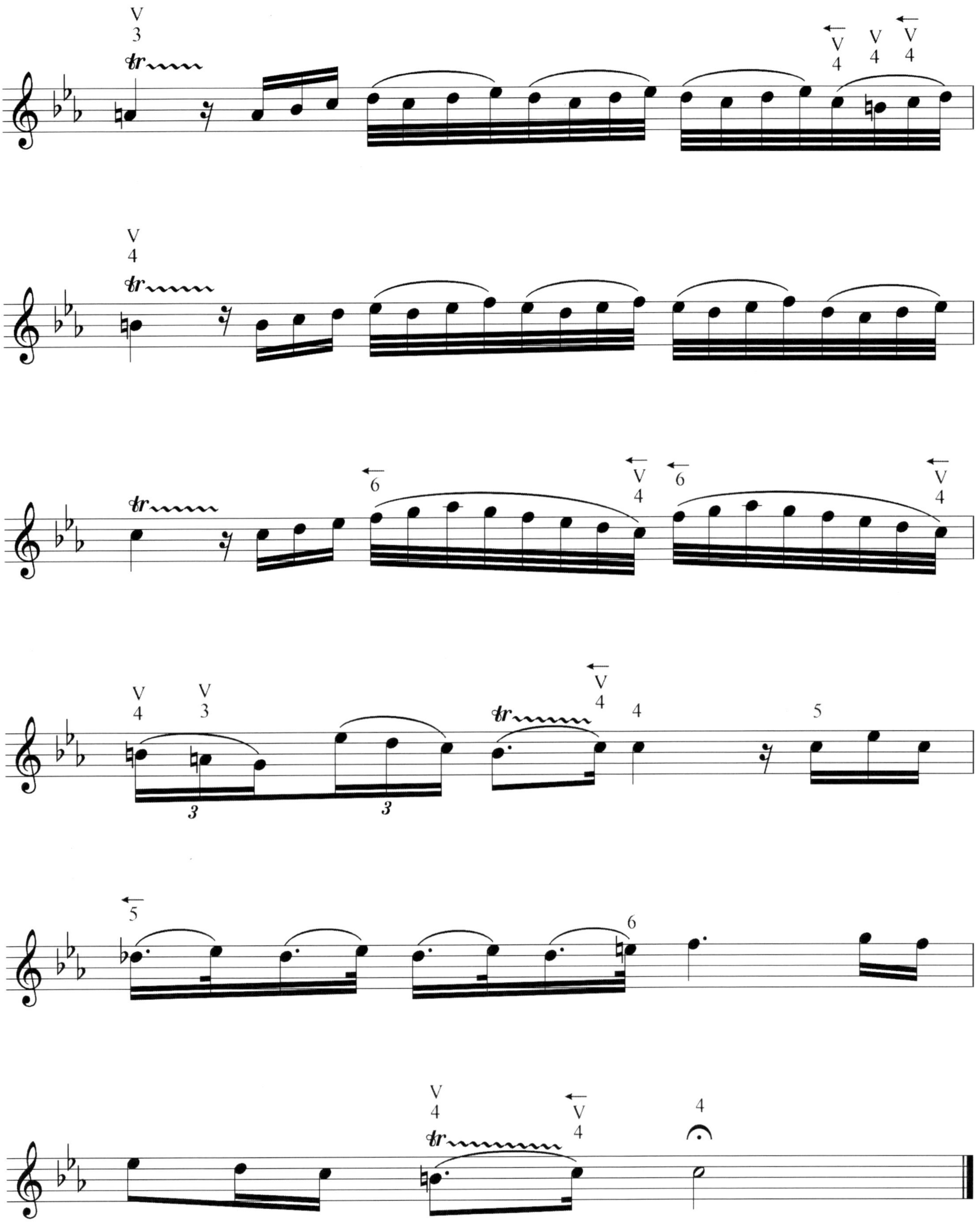

Violin Concerto in A minor

III

Presto

Antonio Vivaldi, Arr. Jiayi He

110
114
122
127
132
139

Oh! Mio Babbino Caro

Giacomo Puccini, Arr. Jiayi He

Serenade

Franz Joseph Haydn
Arranged by Jiayi He

calando
a tempo
espress.

a tempo
poco rall.
dolce
dim.
calando

Zigeunerweisen

(Gypsy Airs)

Pablo de Sarasate, Op. 20
Arranged by Jiayi He

Lento
très passioné
rall.
rit.
rit.
espressivo
dim.
rit.
pressez.

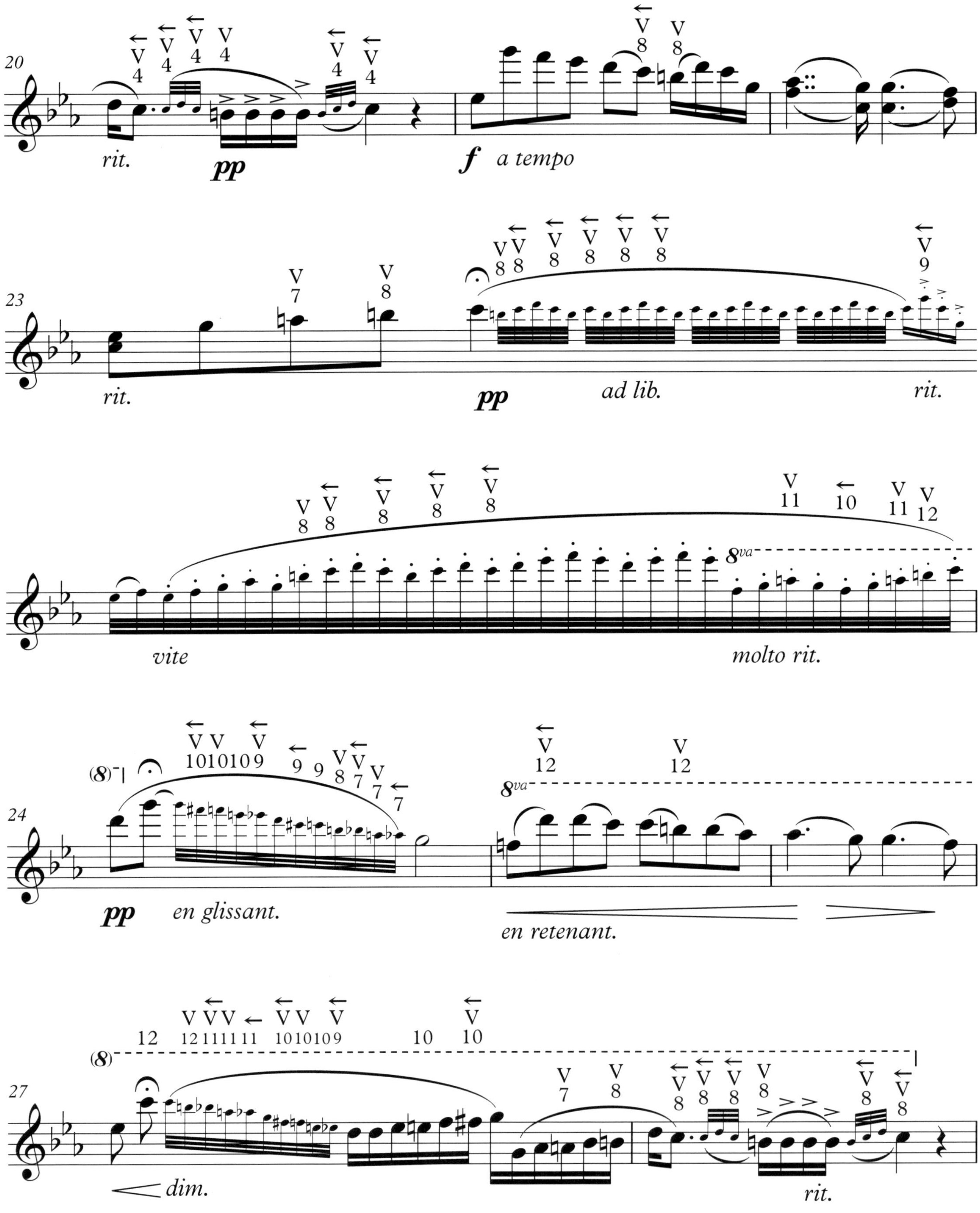
rit.
pp
f
a tempo
rit.
pp
ad lib.
rit.
vite
molto rit.
pp
en glissant.
en retenant.
dim.
rit.

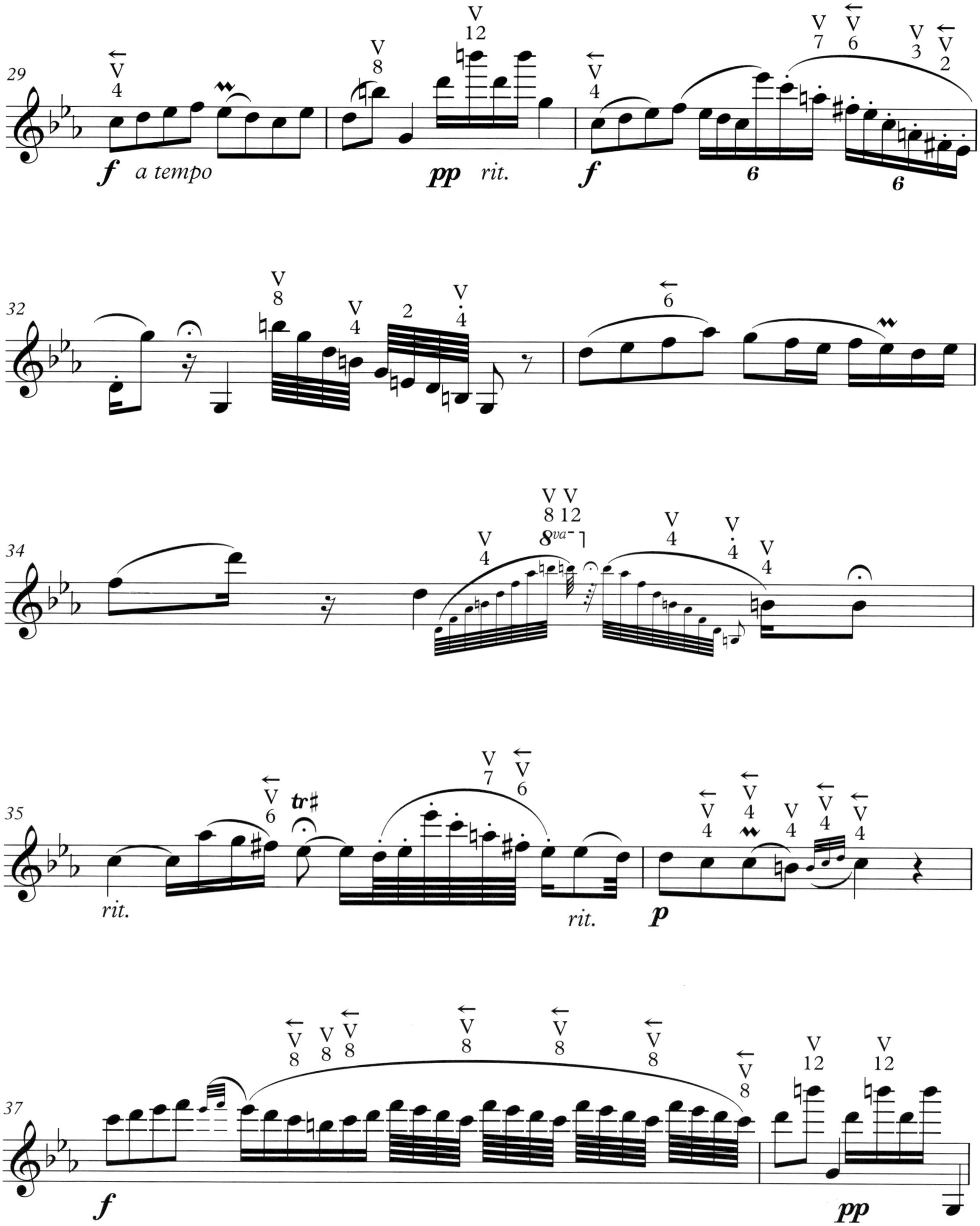

a tempo
rit.
8va
rit.
rit.

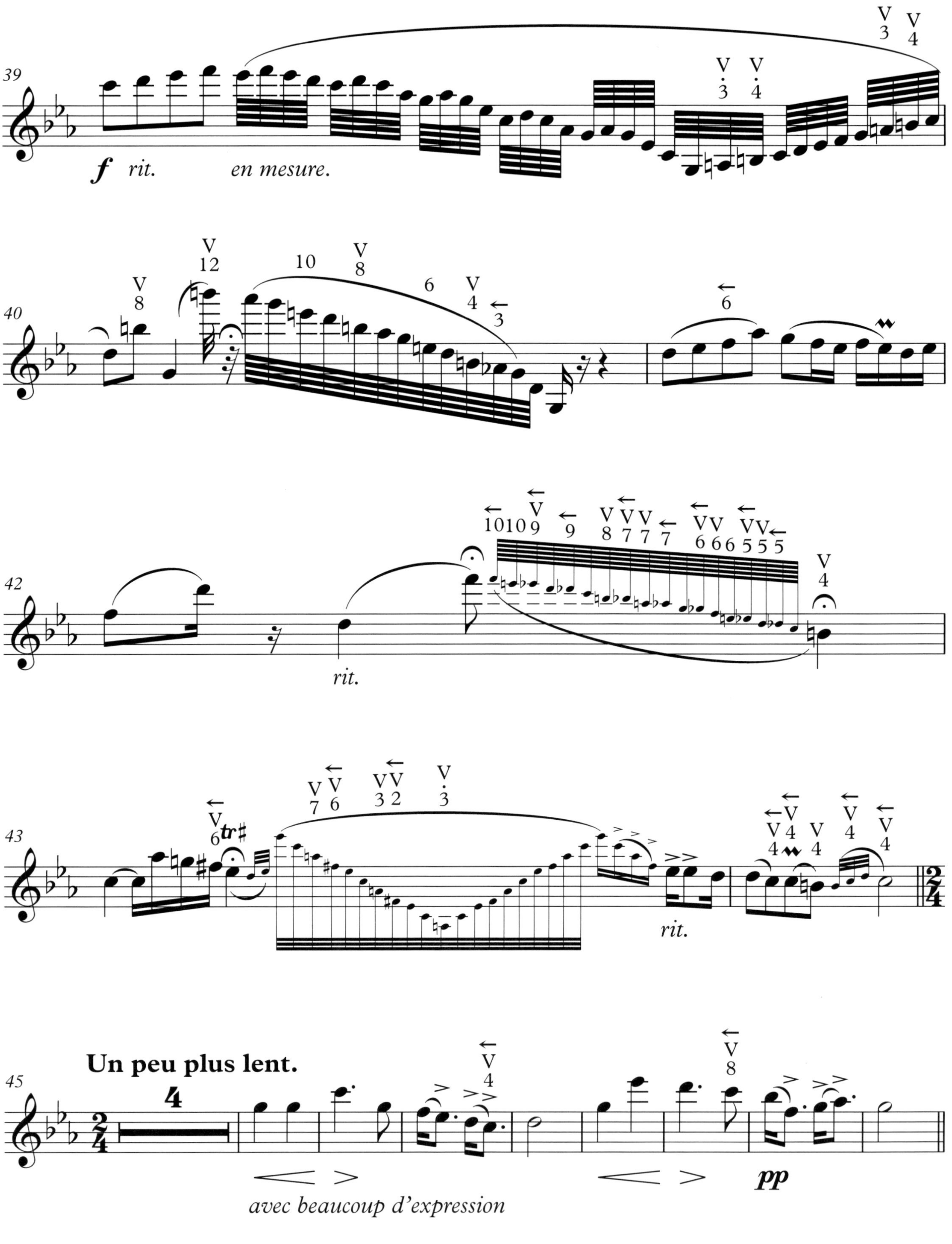
rit.
en mesure.
rit.
rit.
Un peu plus lent.
avec beaucoup d'expression

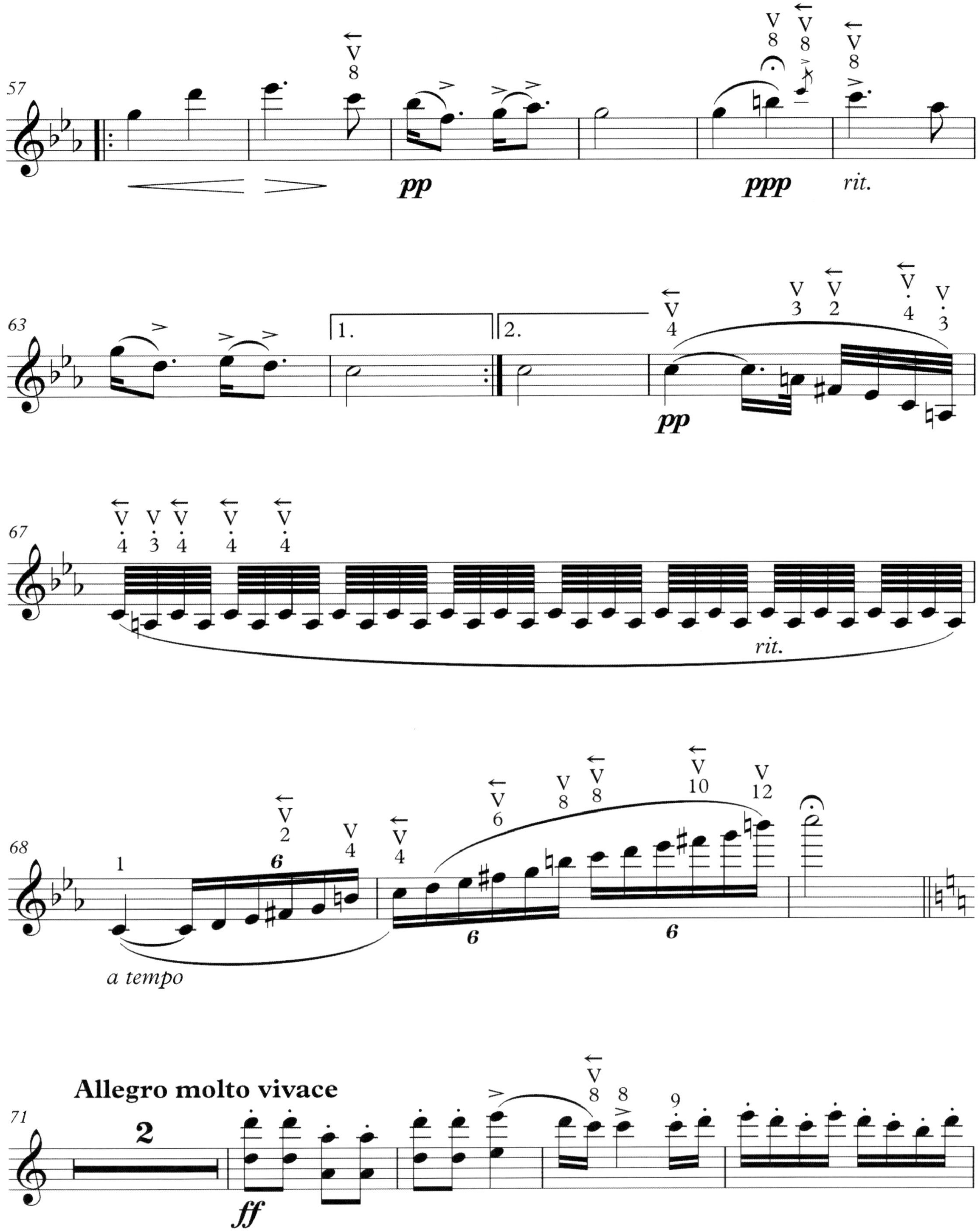
57
pp
ppp
rit.
63
1.
2.
pp
67
rit.
68
a tempo
Allegro molto vivace
71
ff

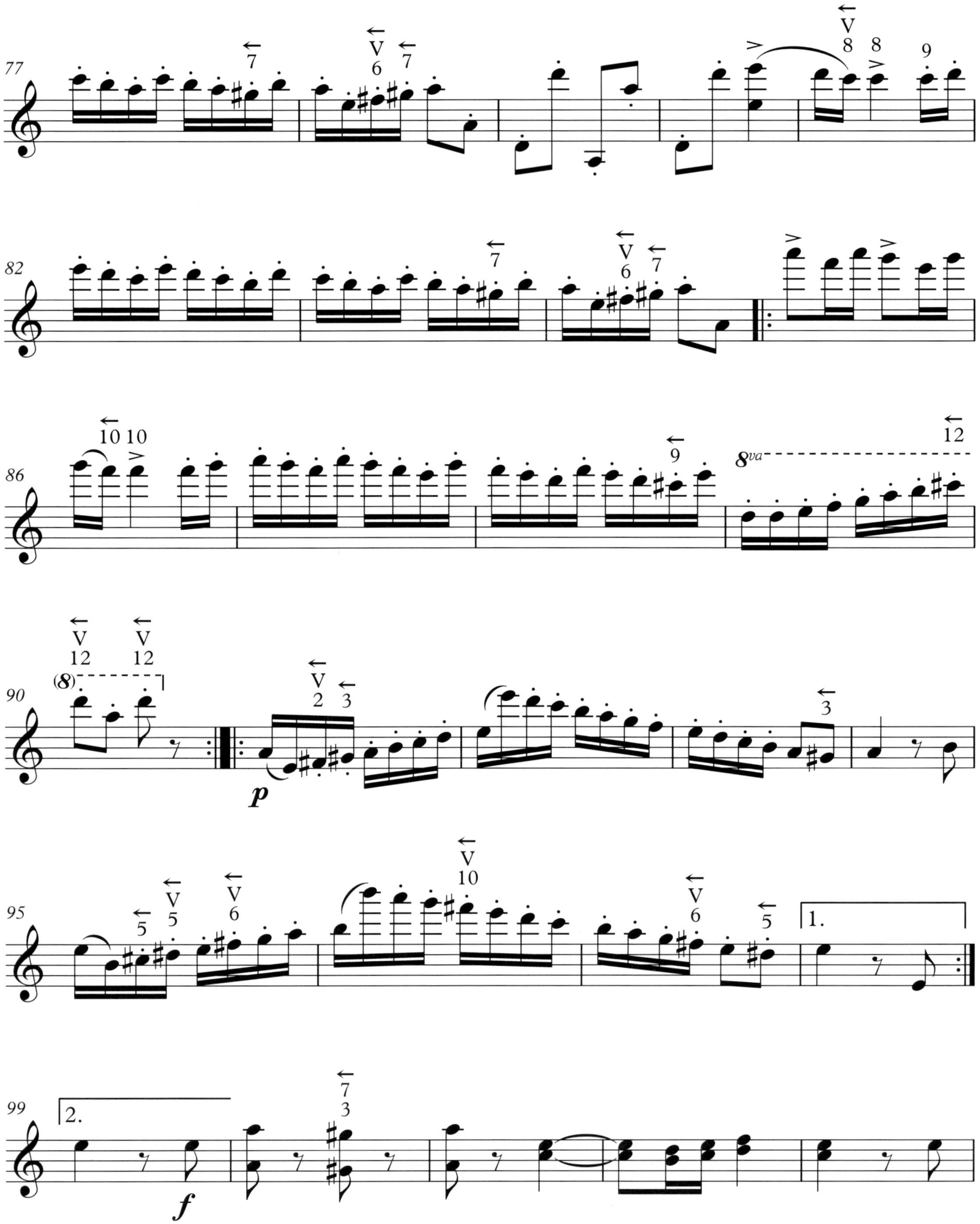
77
82
86
8va
90
(8)
95
1.
99
2.

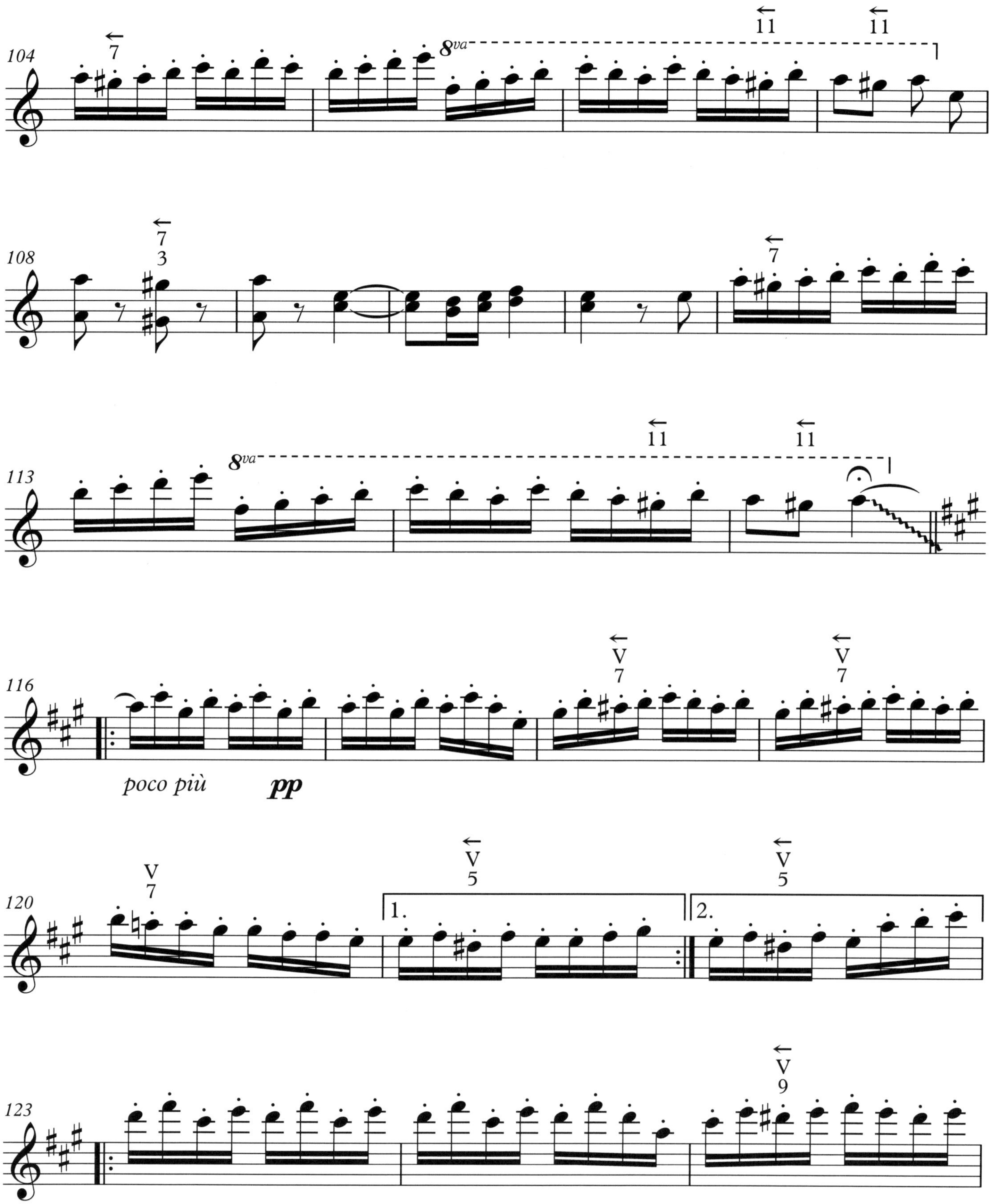
8va
8va
poco più
pp
1.
2.

153
8va
157
(8)
f
163
8va
167
(8)
cresc.
ff

Special Scale Study Section

G Major / E Minor Scales and Arpeggios

G Major

Harmonica tabs by Jiayi He

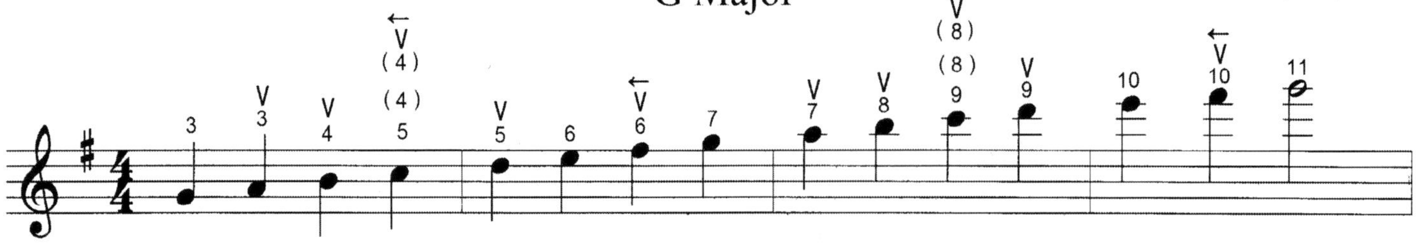

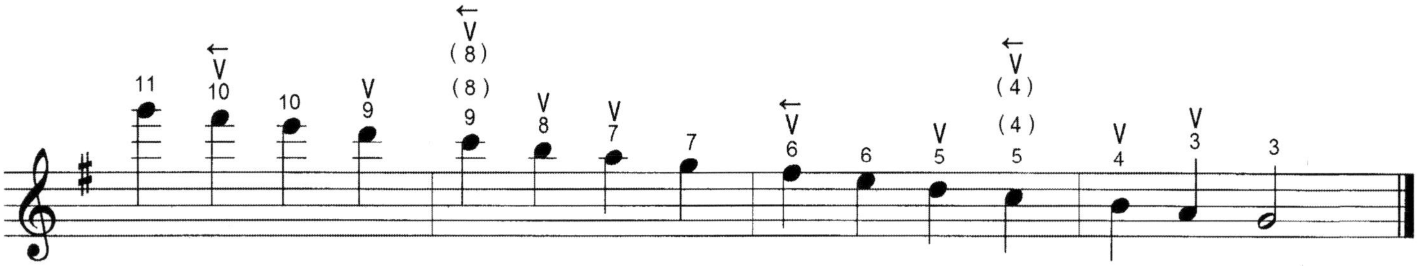

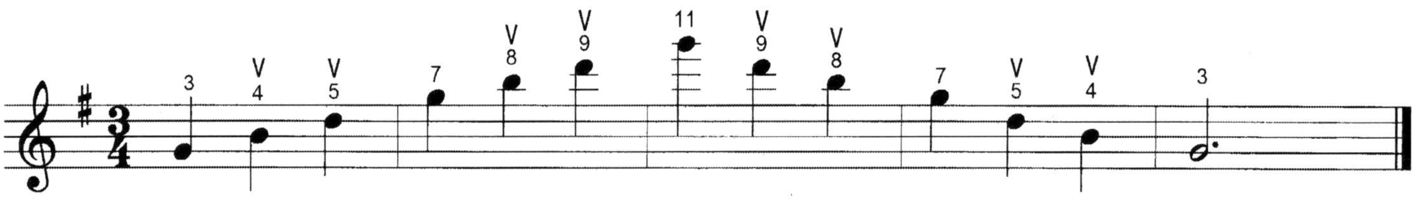

E Minor

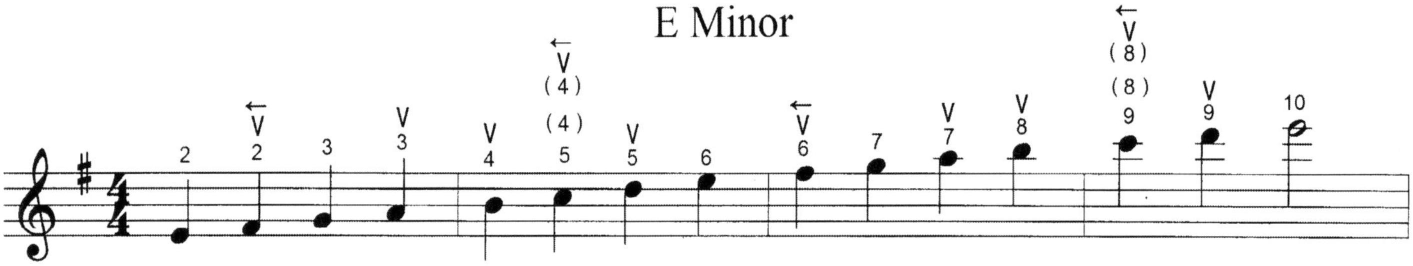

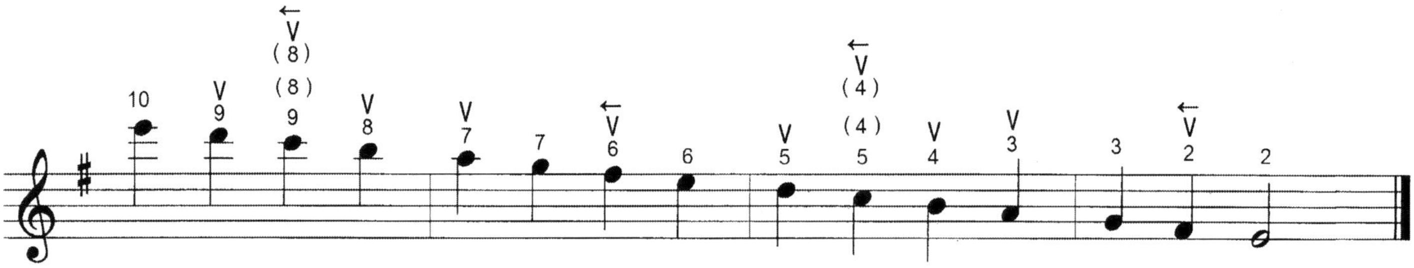

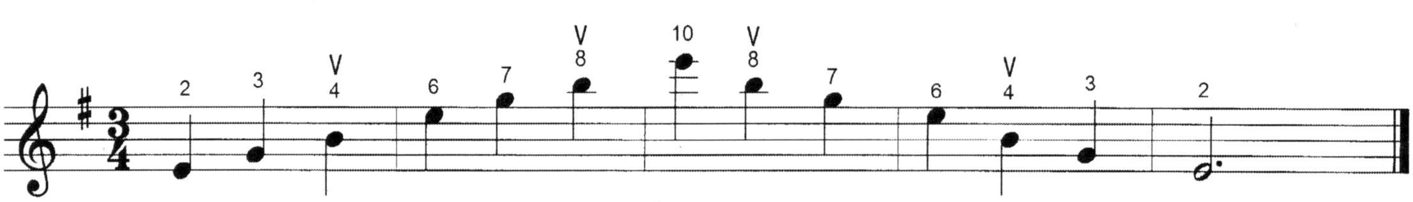

1 to 12 are the holes on the harmonica. V = draw. ← for push in the slide. ( ) = possible options.

Ab Major / F Minor Scales and Arpeggios

Harmonica tabs by Jiayi He

Ab Major

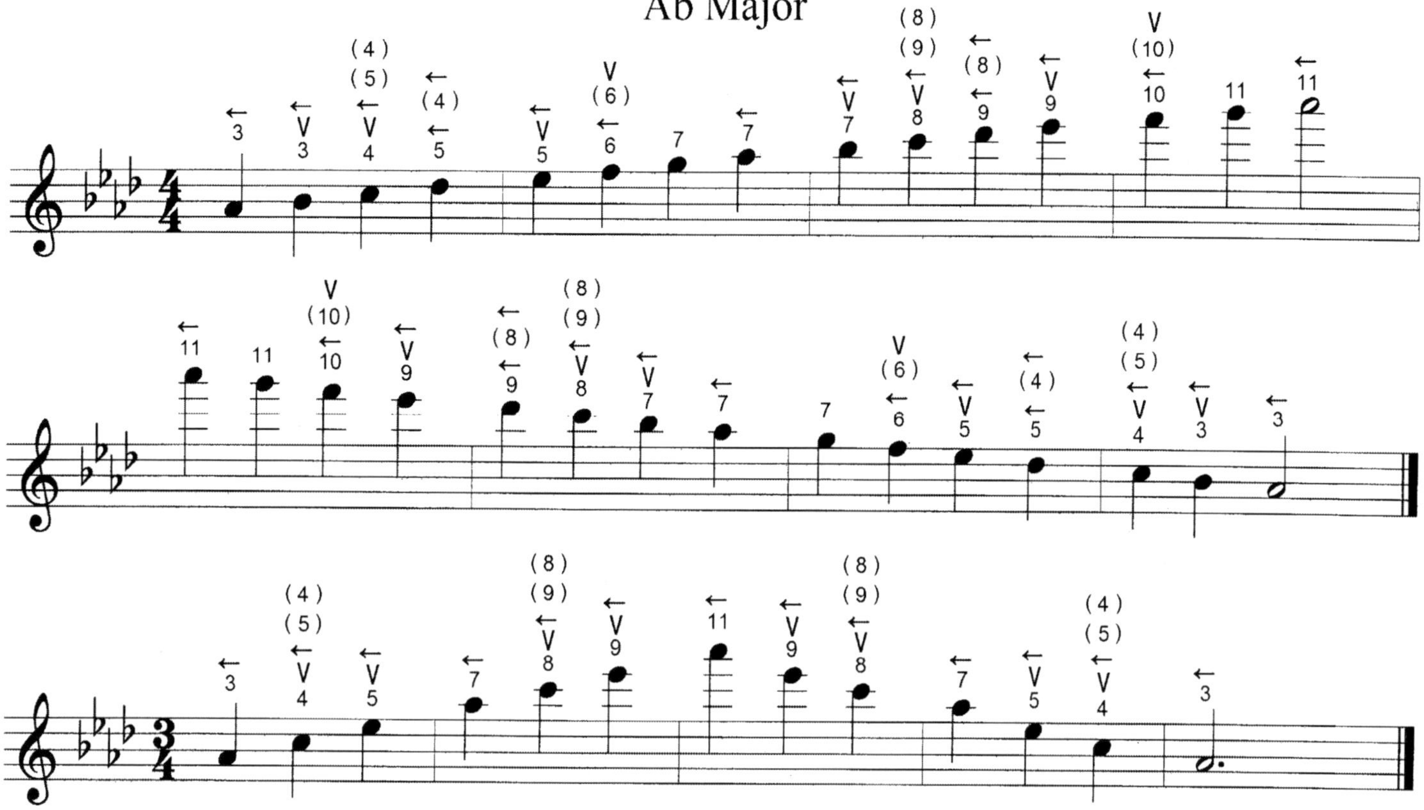

F Minor

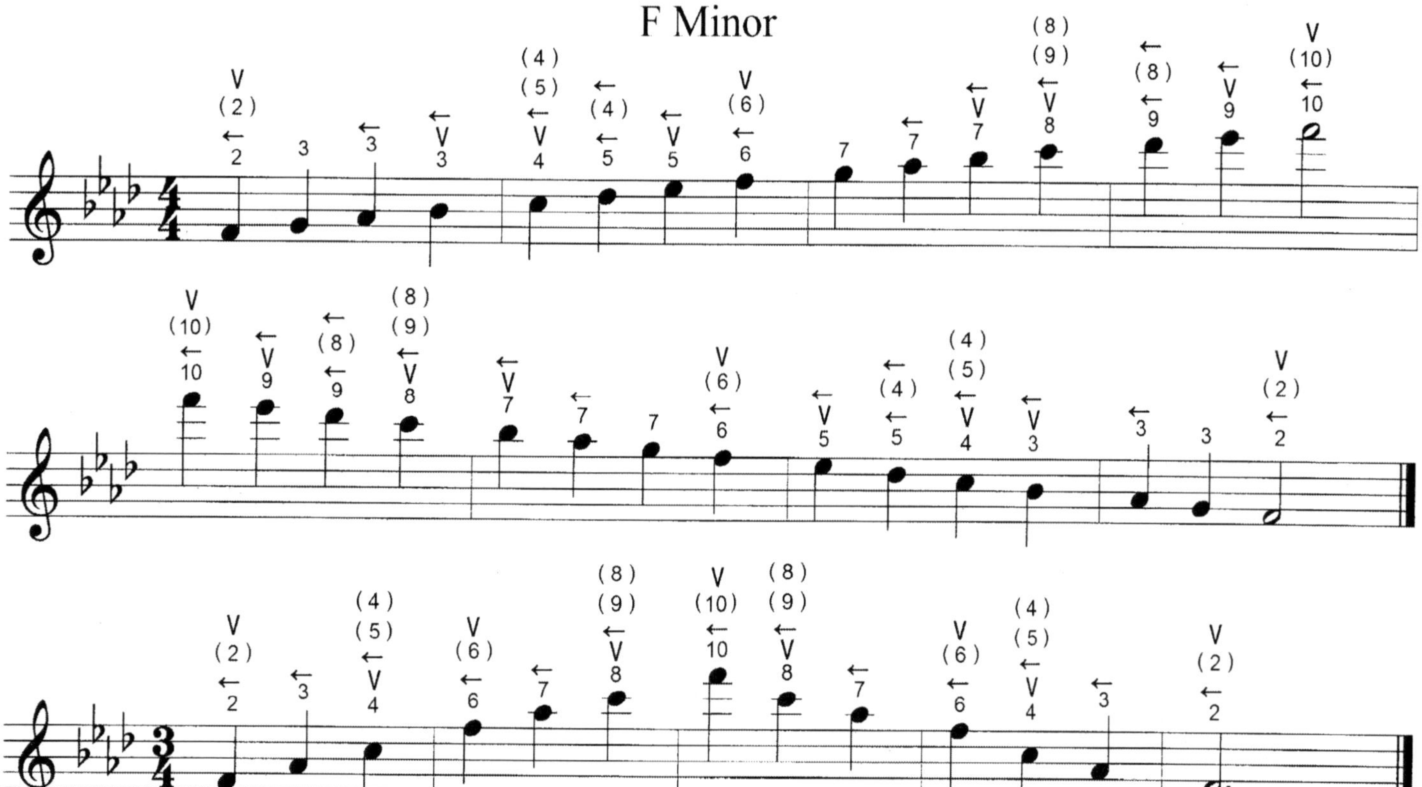

1 to 12 are the holes on the harmonica. V = draw. ← for push in the slide. ( ) = possible options.

A Major / F# Minor Scales and Arpeggios

A Major

Harmonica tabs by Jiayi He

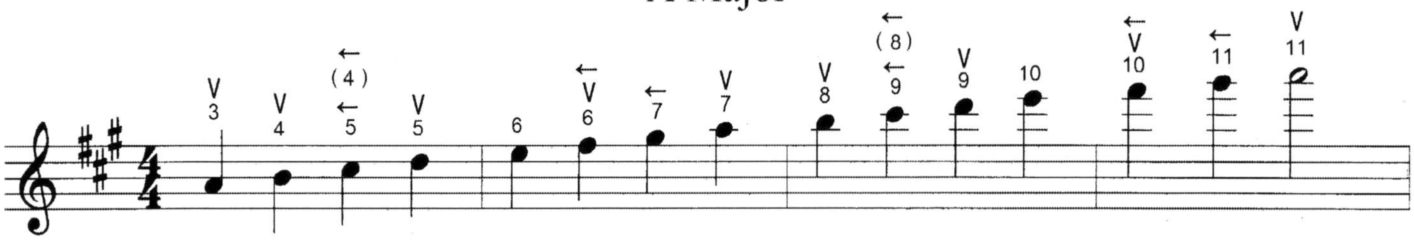

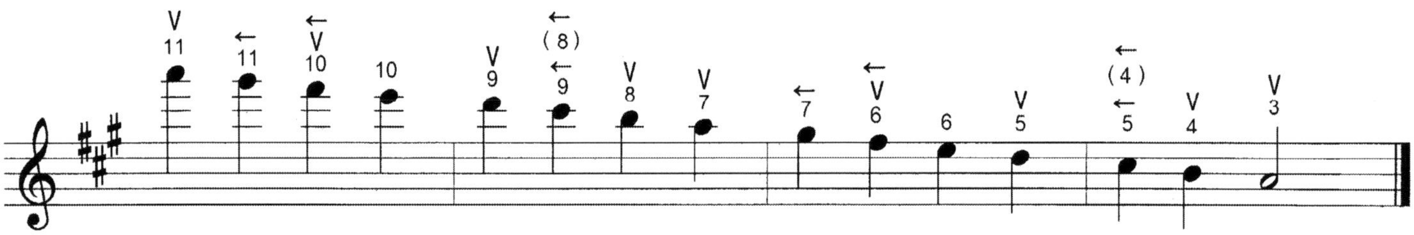

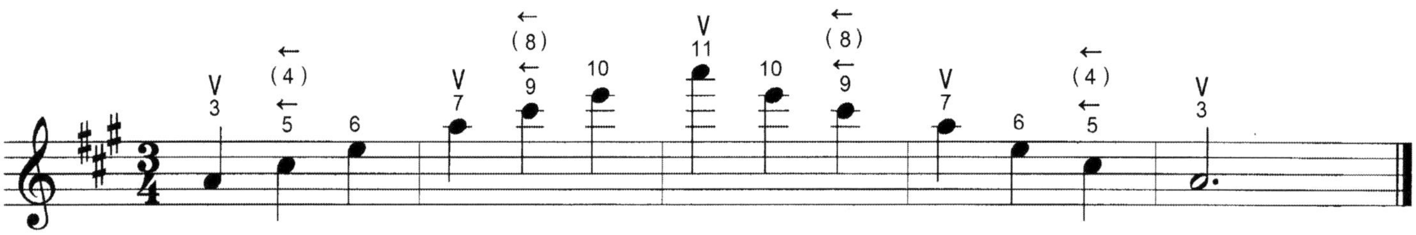

F# Minor

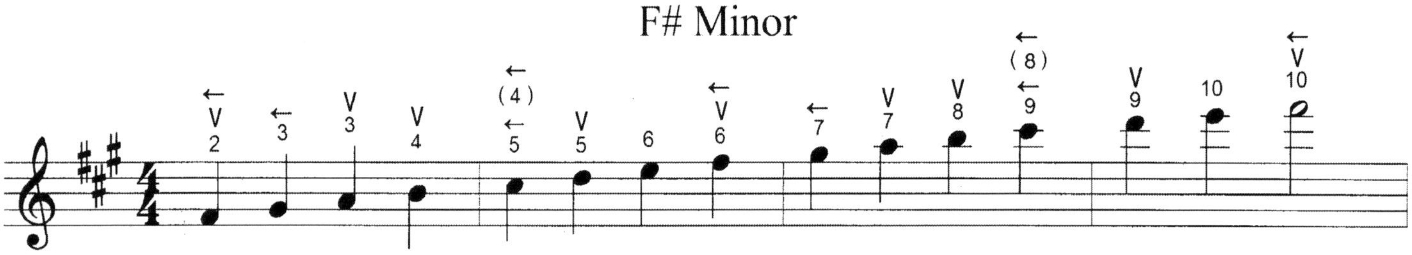

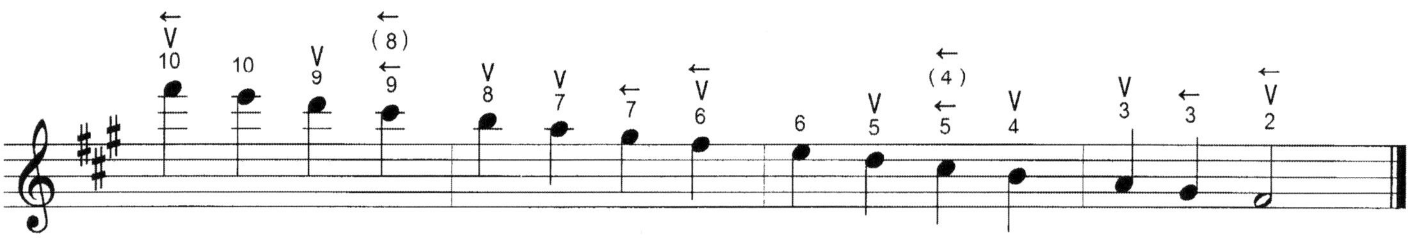

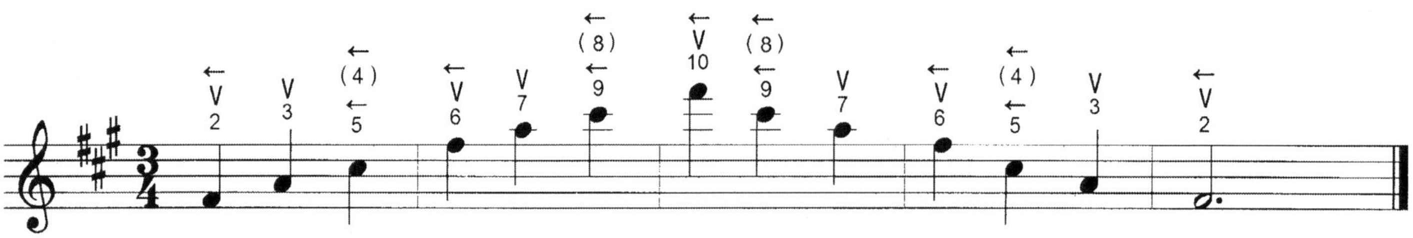

1 to 12 are the holes on the harmonica. V = draw. ← for push in the slide. ( ) = possible options.

Bb Major / G Minor Scales and Arpeggios

Bb Major

Harmonica tabs by Jiayi He

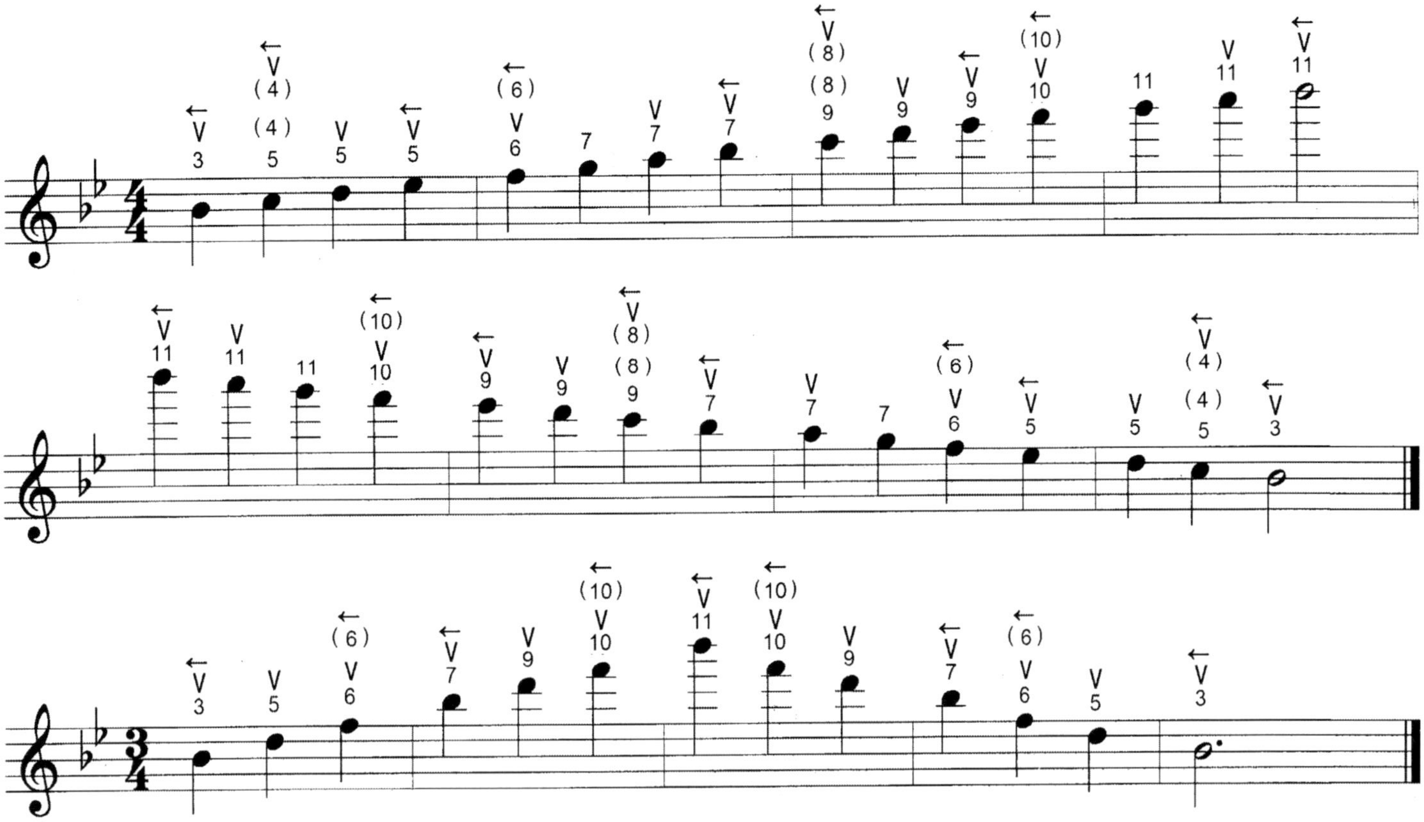

G Minor

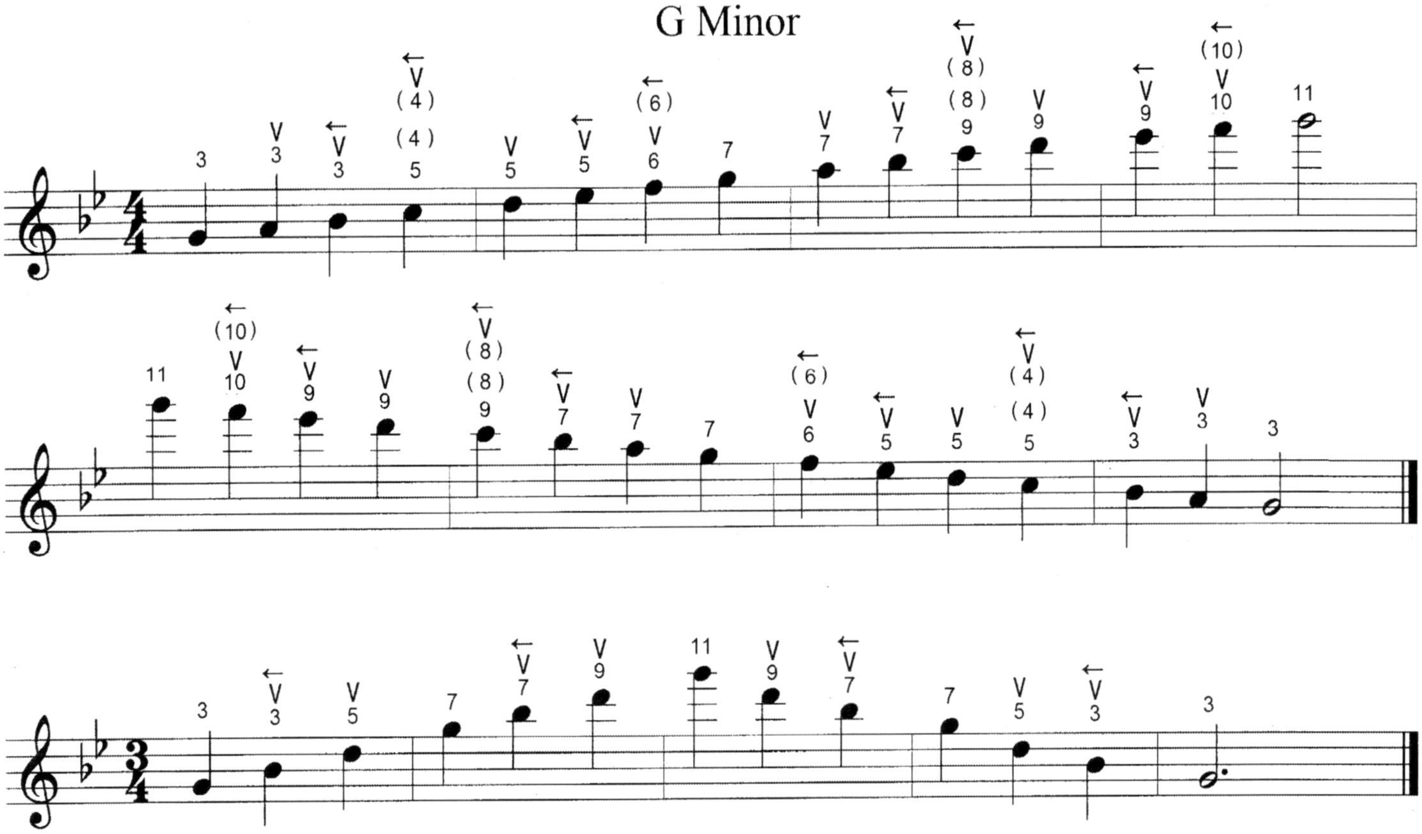

1 to 12 are the holes on the harmonica. V = draw. ← for push in the slide. ( ) = possible options.

B Major / G# Minor Scales and Arpeggios

B Major

Harmonica tabs by Jiayi He

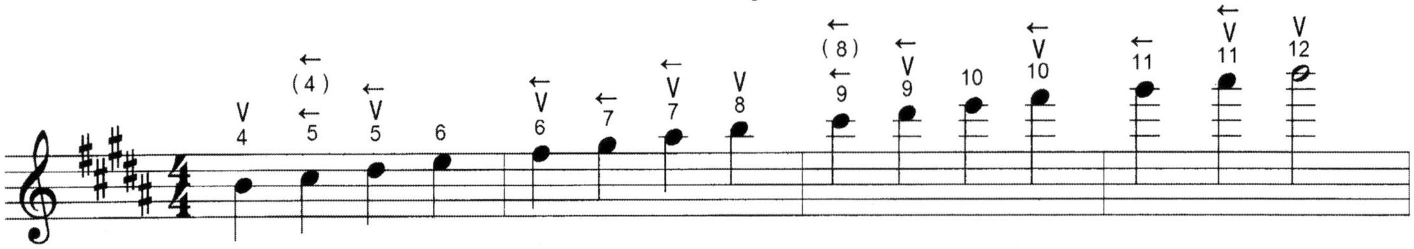

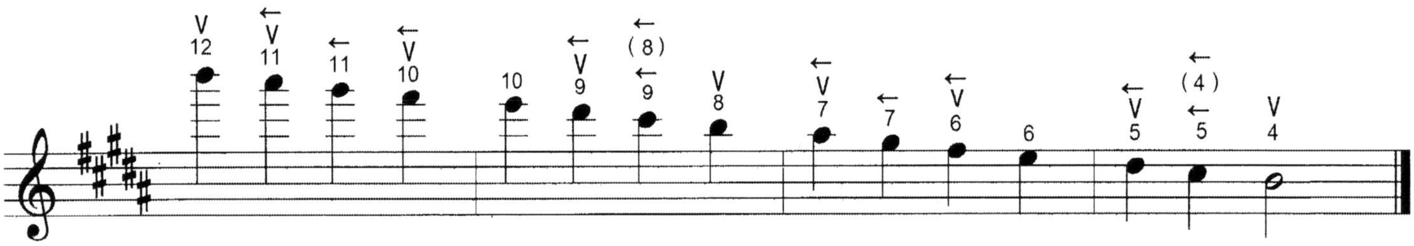

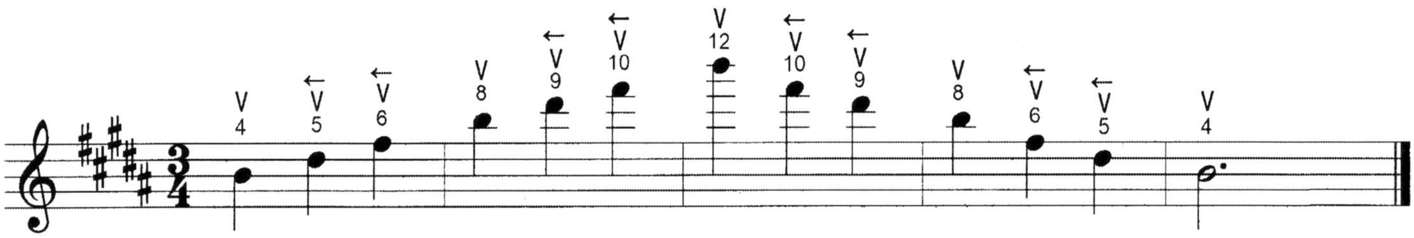

G# Minor

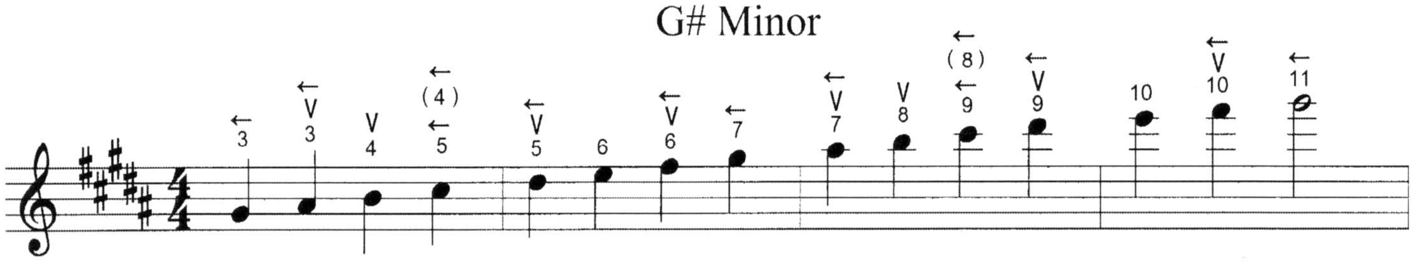

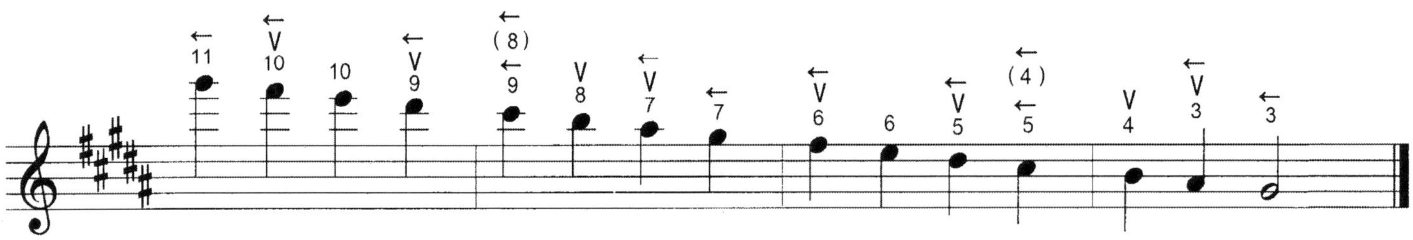

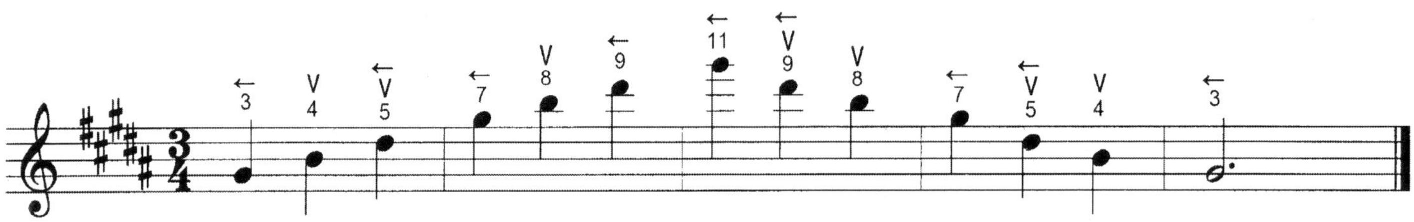

1 to 12 are the holes on the harmonica. V = draw. ← for push in the slide. ( ) = possible options.

C Major / A Minor Scales and Arpeggios

C Major

Harmonica tabs by Jiayi He

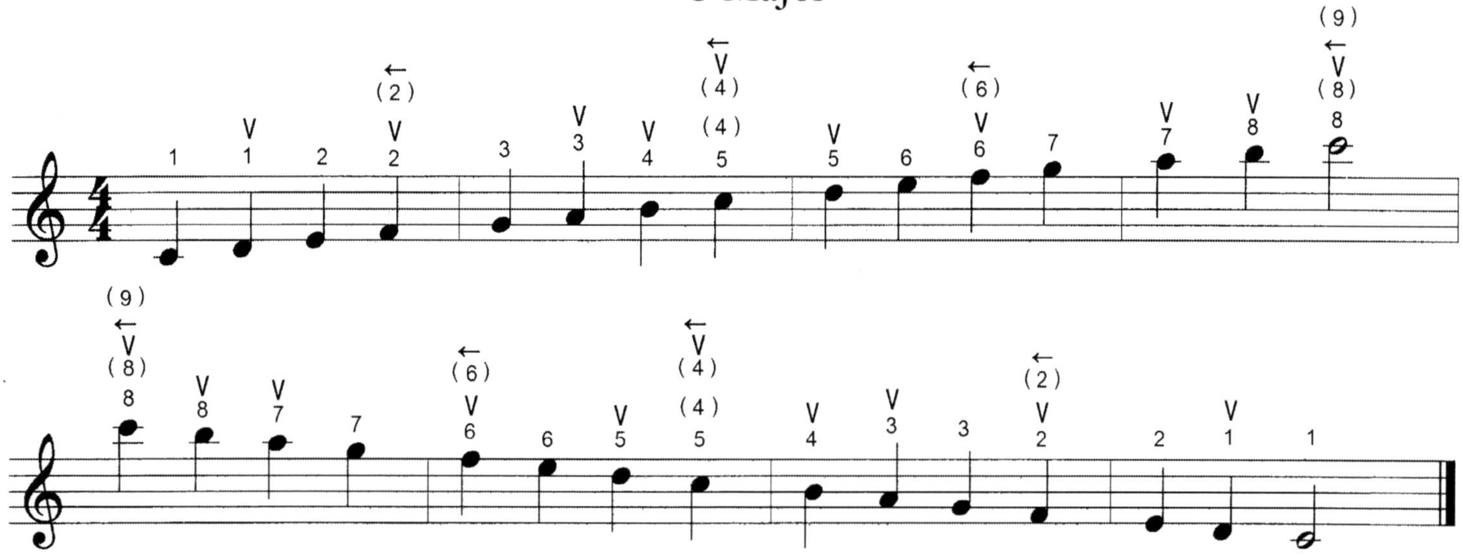

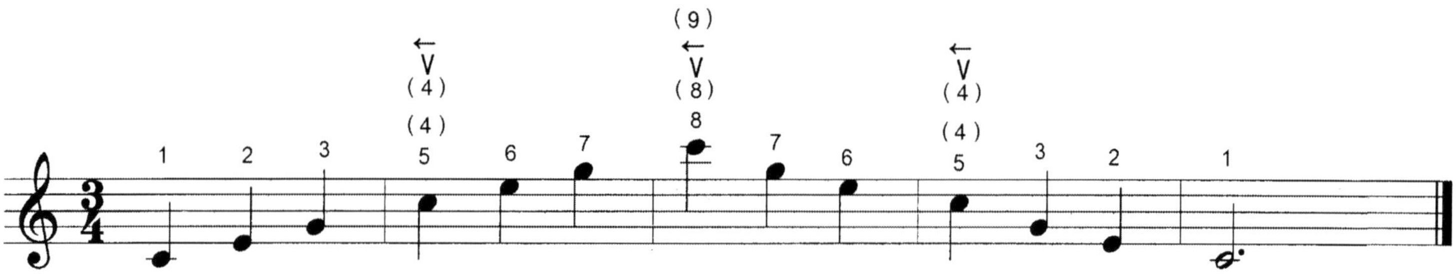

A Minor

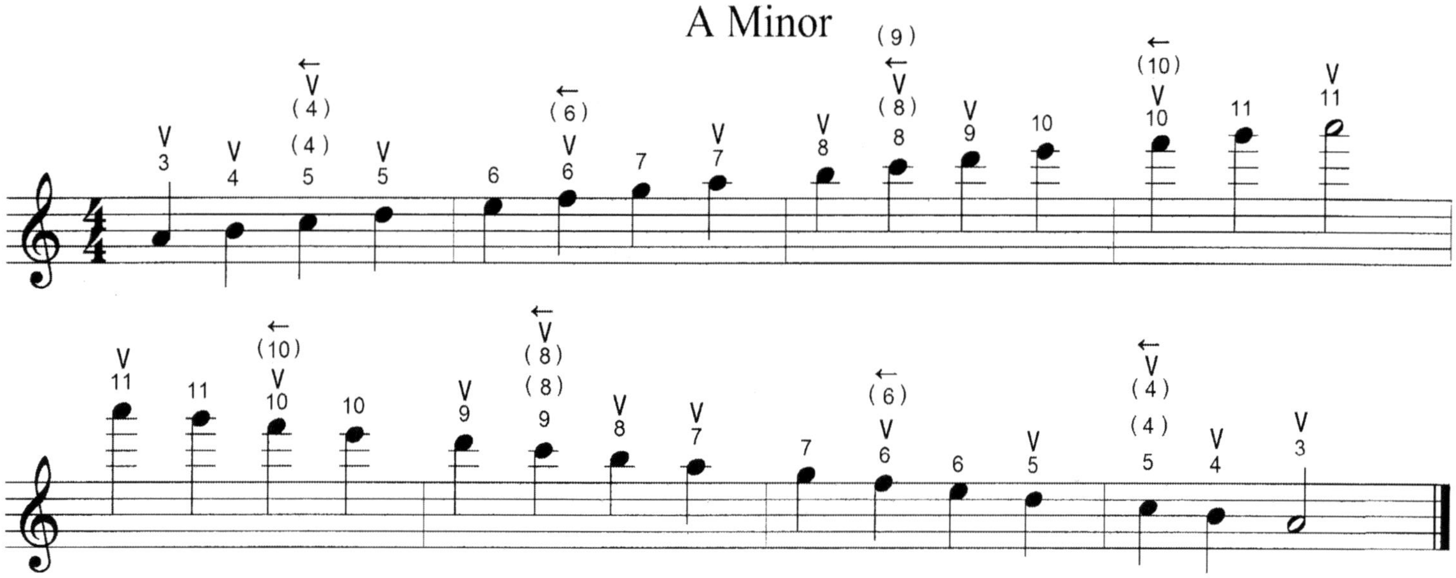

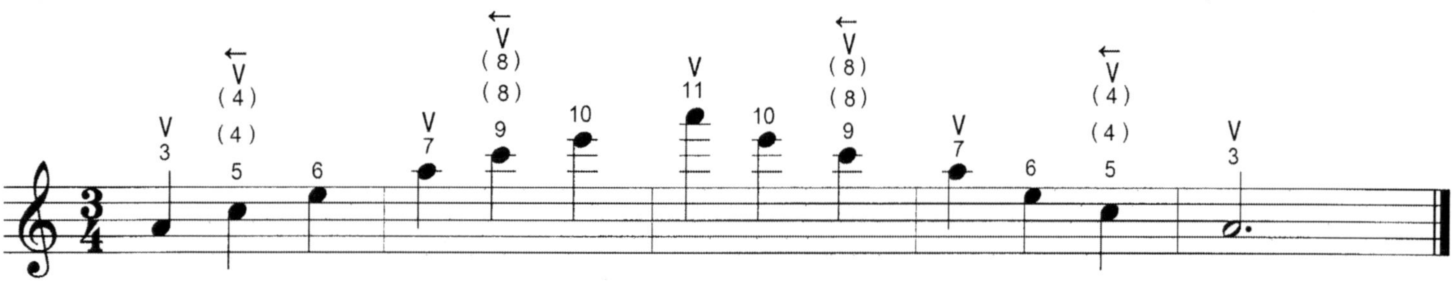

1 to 12 are the holes on the harmonica. V = draw. ← for push in the slide. ( ) = possible options.

Db Major / Bb Minor Scales and Arpeggios

Db Major

Harmonica tabs by Jiayi He

Bb Minor

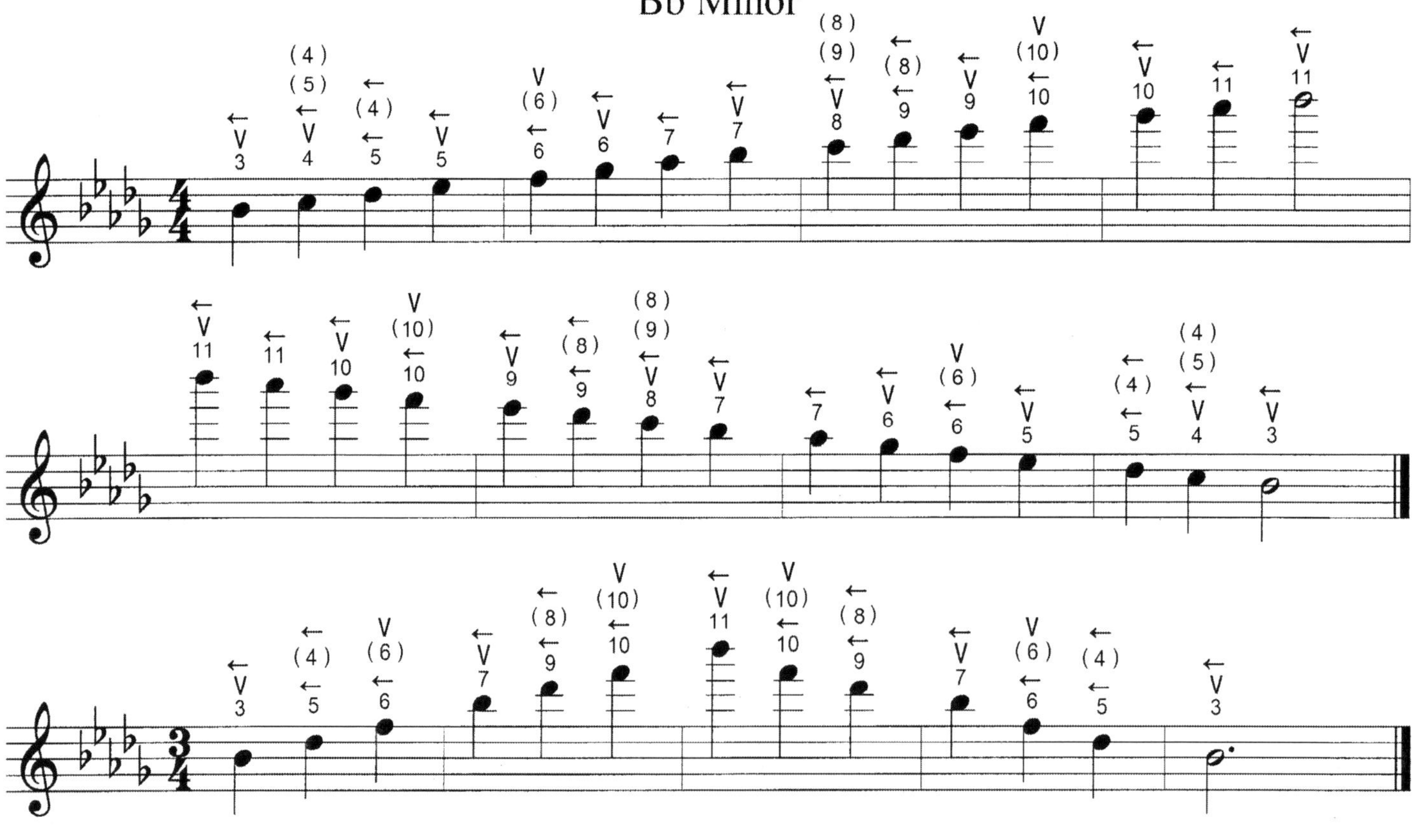

1 to 12 are the holes on the harmonica. V = draw. ← for push in the slide. ( ) = possible options.

D Major / B Minor Scales and Arpeggios

D Major

Harmonica tabs by Jiayi He

B Minor

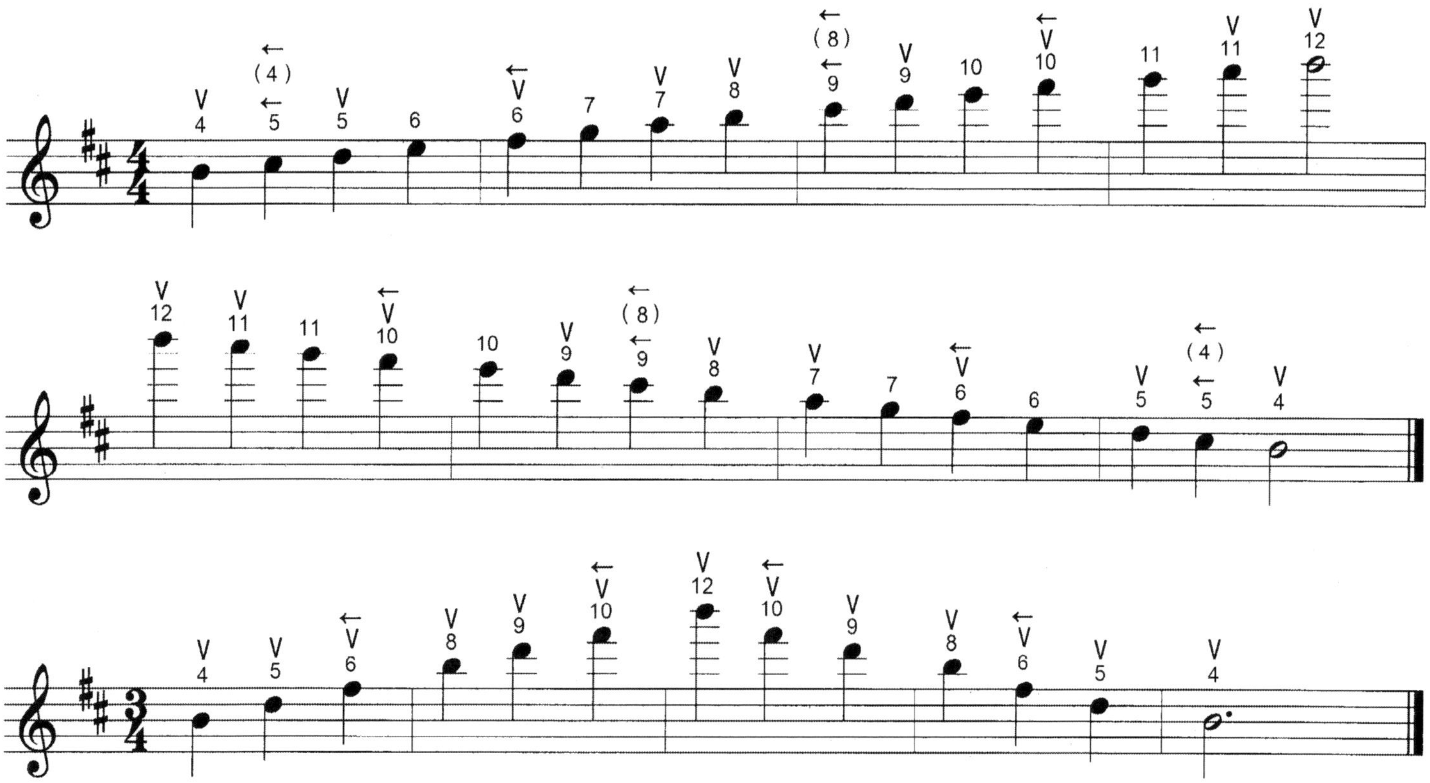

1 to 12 are the holes on the harmonica. V = draw. ← for push in the slide. ( ) = possible options.

Eb Major / C Minor Scales and Arpeggios

Eb Major

Harmonica tabs by Jiayi He

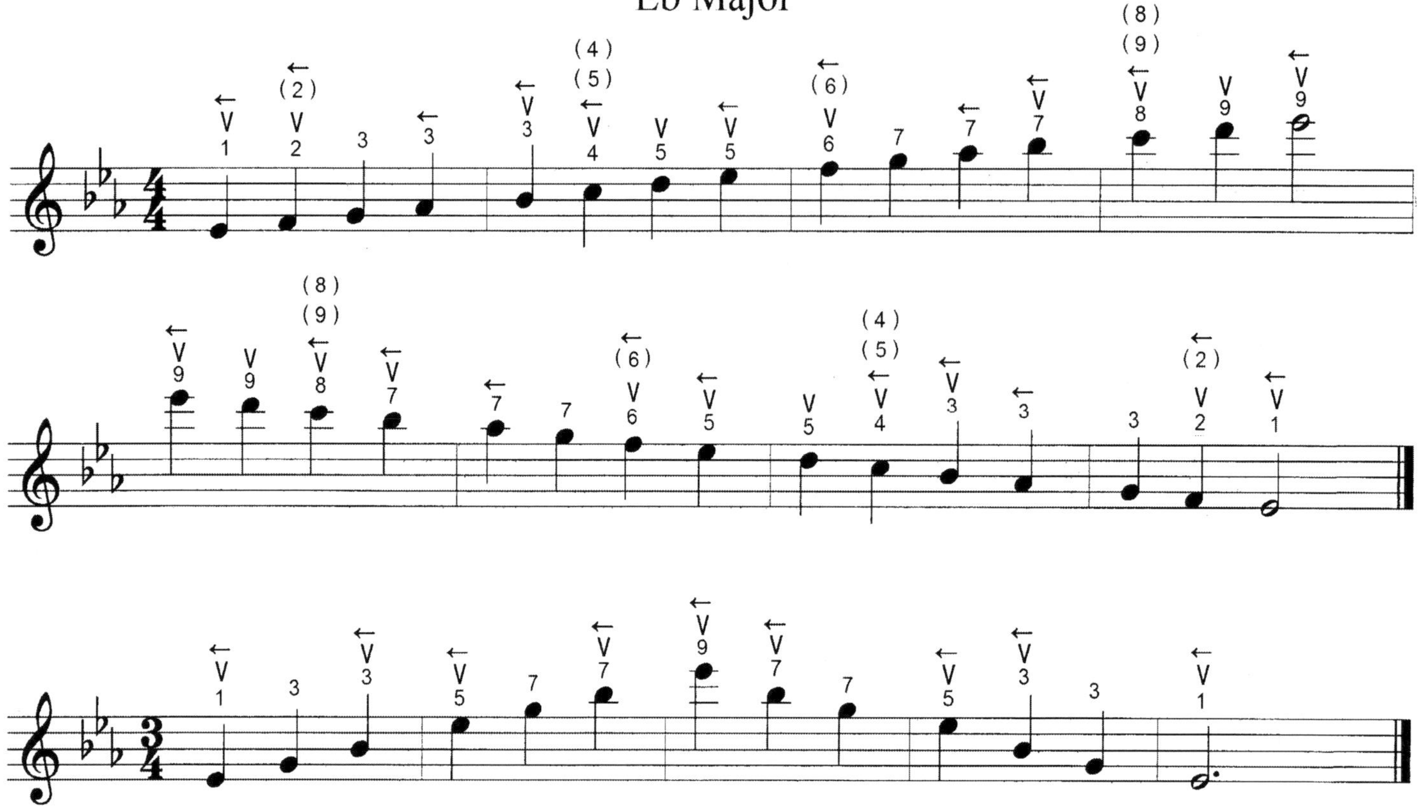

C Minor

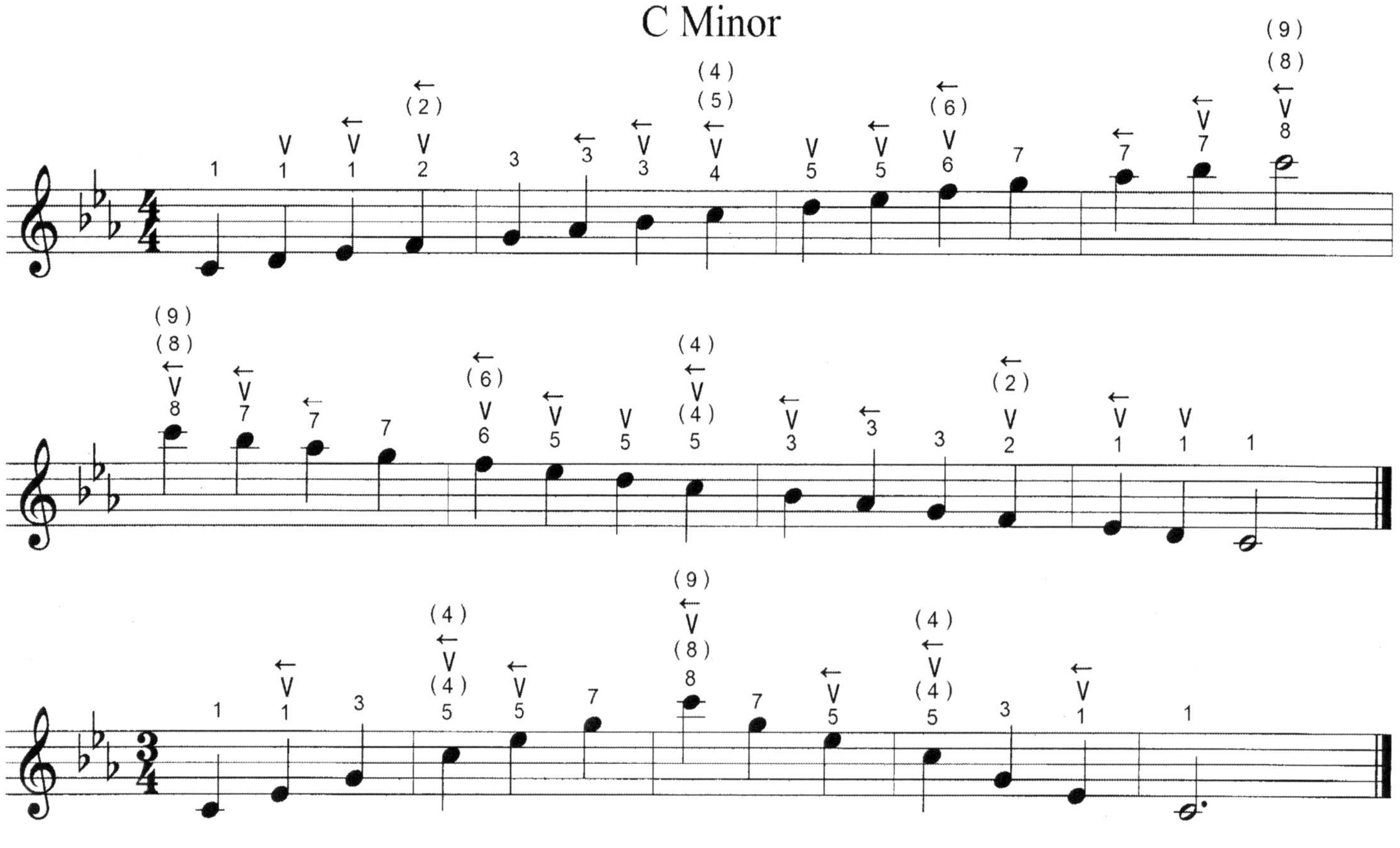

1 to 12 are the holes on the harmonica. V = draw. ← for push in the slide. ( ) = possible options.

E Major / C# Minor Scales and Arpeggios

E Major

Harmonica tabs by Jiayi He

C# Minor

1 to 12 are the holes on the harmonica. V = draw. ← for push in the slide. ( ) = possible options.

F Major / D Minor Scales and Arpeggios

Harmonica tabs by Jiayi He

F Major

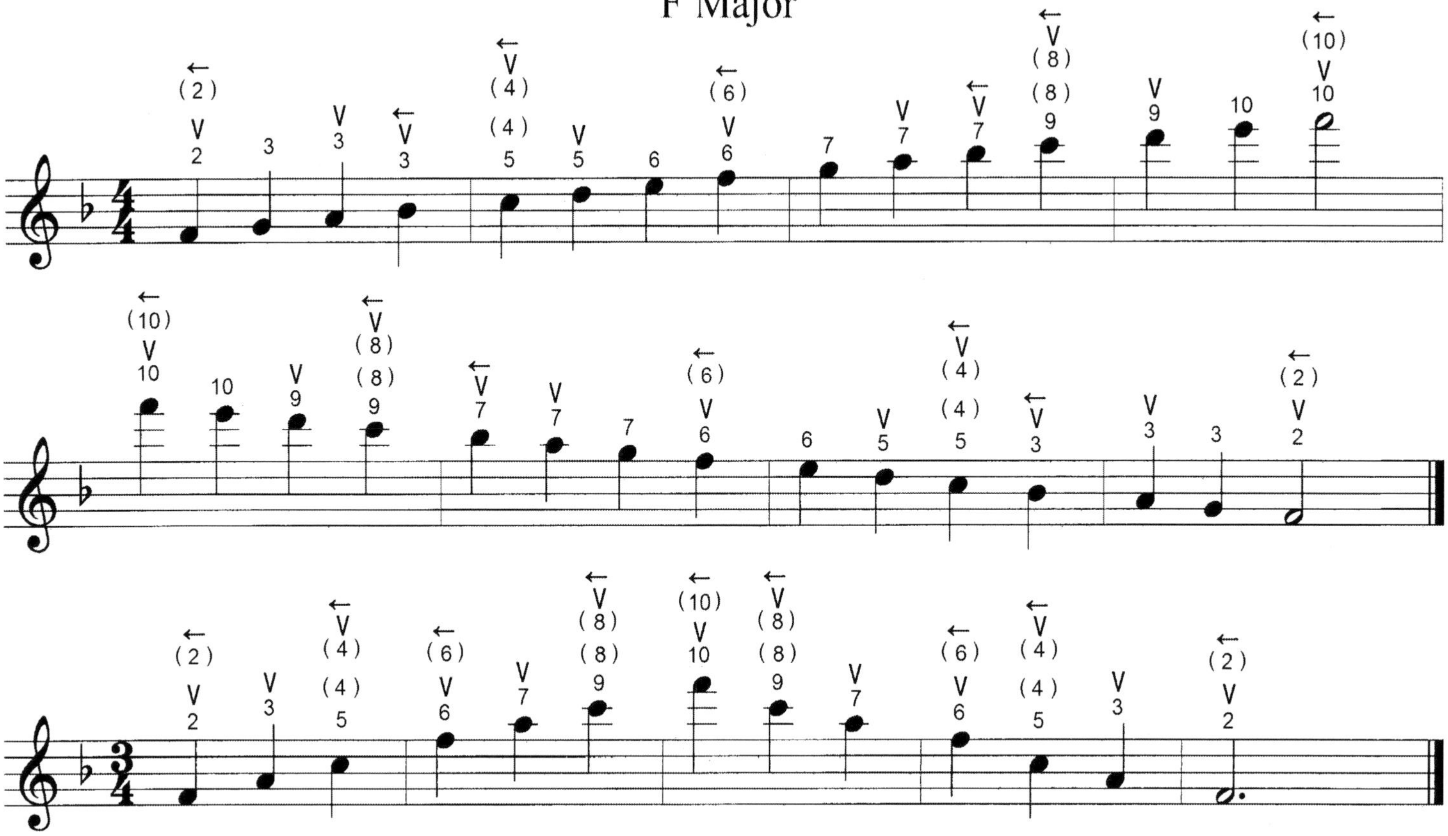

D Minor

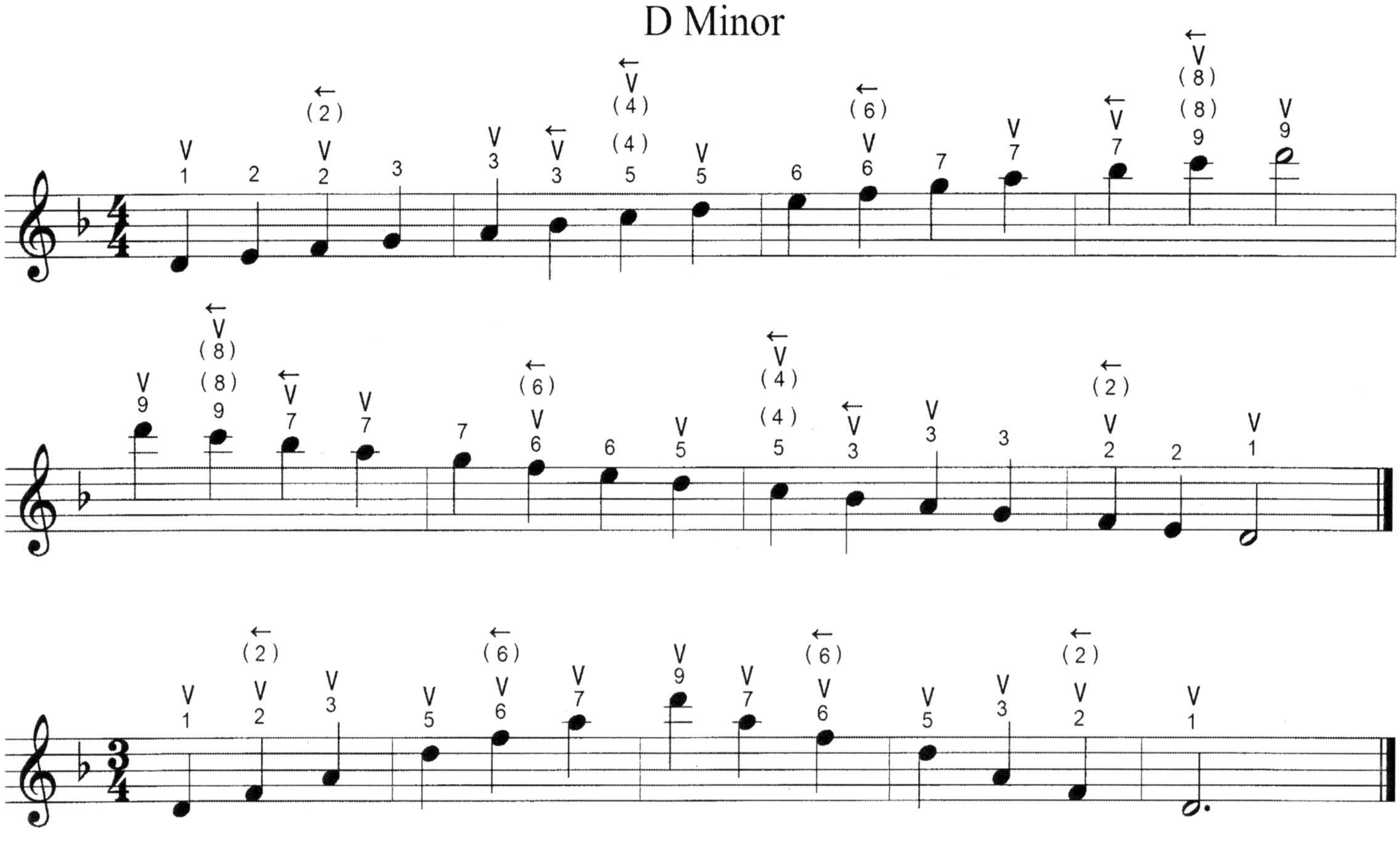

1 to 12 are the holes on the harmonica. V = draw. ← for push in the slide. ( ) = possible options.

F# Major / D# Minor Scales and Arpeggios

Harmonica tabs by Jiayi He

F# Major

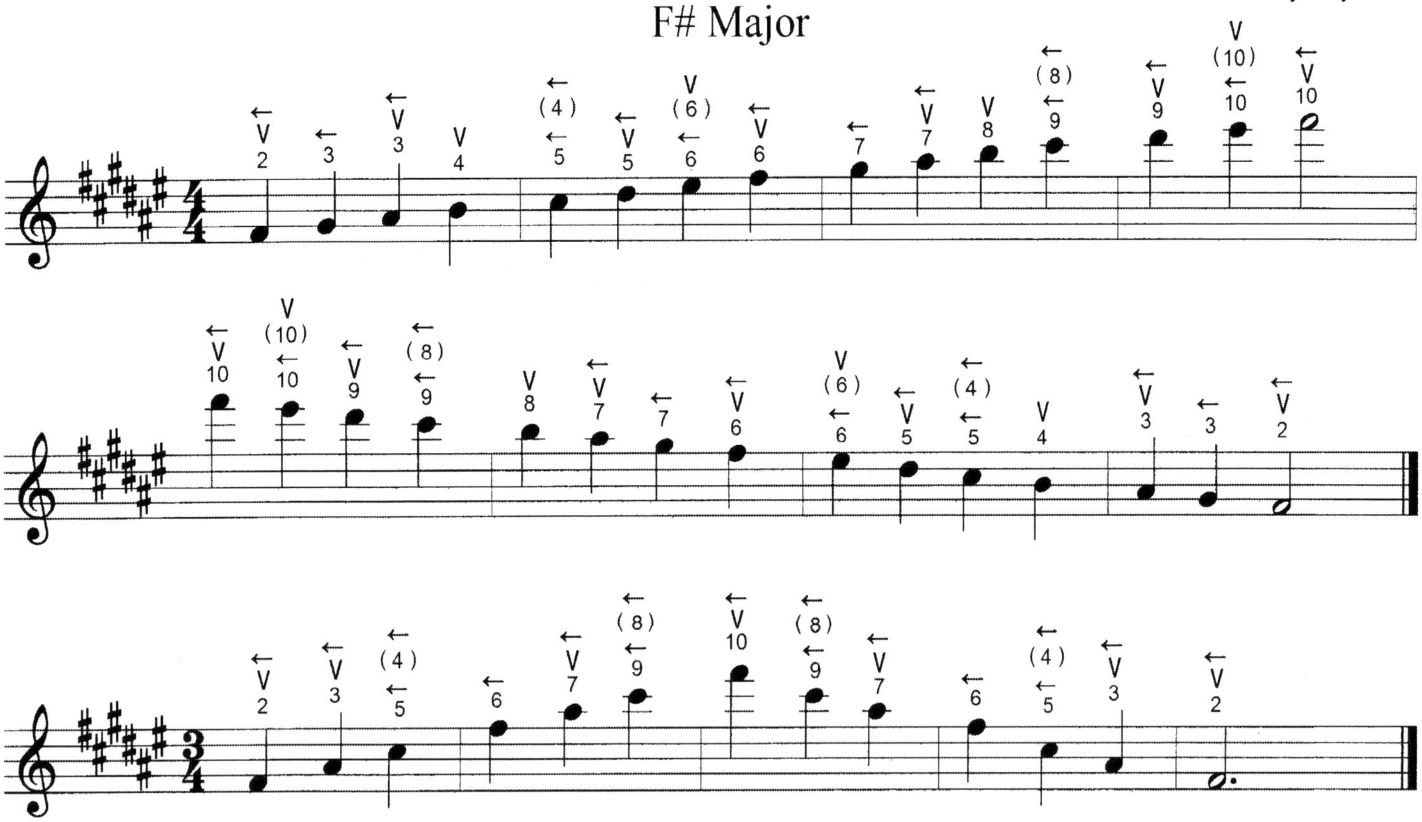

D# Minor

1 to 12 are the holes on the harmonica. V = draw. ← for push in the slide. ( ) = possible options.

About the Author

Jiayi He, a world-class harmonica virtuoso, has received numerous awards at international festivals and competitions in England, Germany, Israel, Japan and the United States. He has served as a member of the judging committees in the Asia-Pacific Harmonica Competitions held in Taiwan, Malaysia, Hong Kong, Hangzhou, Korea and Singapore. Jiayi has appeared as a soloist with orchestras worldwide. He has appeared on TV stations including NBC, New 12 Long Island, Queens Public Television, Sinovison and Sino Television. Jiayi has recorded harmonica music for a number of movies and radio stations in addition to his compact discs. Jiayi has been a soloist at Carnegie Hall, Lincoln Center, Shea Stadium, General Assembly Hall at United Nations and other premier venues. Former New York City Mayor Bloomberg attended his harmonica seminar held at the "Harmonica Mass Appeal 2012". Jiayi currently serves on the harmonica faculty of the Turtle Bay Music School in New York City. Jiayi has been teaching these remarkable solo harmonica arrangements at the Turtle Bay Music School since 2002. Most of the pieces in this book may be viewed at: *www.youtube.com/hHarmonica.*